DK EYEWITNESS BOOKS

UNIVERSE

Hubble Space Telescope

High-energy particle tracks

Magellan Venus orbiter

Jupiter and its moon Io

Martian Volcano

The surface of Mars

Bust of Jupiter

DK EYEWITNESS BOOKS

Chandra X-ray satellite

UNIVERSE

Written by
ROBIN KERROD

A DK Publishing Book

Core of a quasar

Mars

Spectroscope

DK

LONDON, NEW YORK, MUNICH,
MELBOURNE, and DELHI

Project editor Giles Sparrow
Art editor Tim Brown
Senior editor Kitty Blount
Senior art editor Martin Wilson
Managing editor Andrew Macintyre
Managing art editor Jane Thomas
Category Publisher Linda Martin
Art director Simon Webb
Production Erica Rosen
Picture research Sean Hunter
DTP Designer Siu Yin Ho

This Eyewitness ® Guide has been conceived by
Dorling Kindersley Limited and Editions Gallimard

First American Edition, 2003
03 04 05 06 07 10 9 8 7 6 5 4 3 2 1

Published in the United States by
DK Publishing, Inc.
375 Hudson Street
New York, New York 10014

A Cataloging-in-Publication record for this book is
available from the Library of Congress.

ISBN 0 7894 9238 5

Color reproduction by
Colourscan, Singapore
Printed in China by Toppan

See our complete
product line at
www.dk.com

Very Large Array
radio telescope

Earth

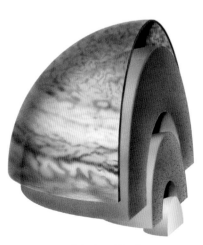

Sunrise at Stonehenge

Inside a supergiant star

Interior of Jupiter

Contents

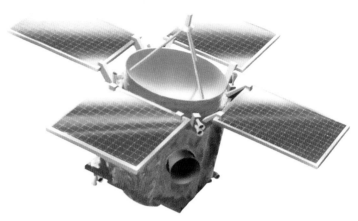

What is the Universe?

THE UNIVERSE IS EVERYTHING THAT EXISTS—today, in the past, and in the future. It is the immensity of space, populated by innumerable galaxies of stars and permeated with light and other radiation. When we look up into the blackness of the night sky, we are peering deep into the fathomless depths of the Universe. Although the stars we see are all trillions of miles away, they are actually close neighbors, because the Universe is unimaginably vast. Humans have been fascinated with the starry heavens from the earliest times, and have been studying them systematically for at least 5,000 years. But although astronomy is probably the oldest science, it has changed continually throughout its history.

SPACESHIP EARTH
The *Apollo 8* astronauts were the first people to see our planet floating alone in the Universe, as they headed for the Moon in 1968. Other astronauts had remained too close to Earth to see the whole planet. It is Spaceship Earth, a beautiful, cloud-flecked, azure world, which is the only place we know where there is life. Profoundly important to us Earthlings, no doubt, but completely insignificant in the Universe as a whole.

"The history of astronomy is a history of receding horizons."

EDWIN HUBBLE
Discoverer of galaxies beyond our own

ANCIENT ASTRONOMERS
Around 4,000 years ago, the ancient Britons had enough astronomical knowledge to build what some consider the first observatory— Stonehenge. In its circles of huge megaliths and smaller standing stones, there were alignments that marked critical positions of the Sun and Moon during the year. Many other ancient monuments around the world also have astronomical alignments.

Babylonian astrological tablet

ASTROLOGY
The priests of ancient Babylon looked to the skies for good and bad signs that they thought might affect the people and matters of state. The idea that what happened in the heavens could affect human lives formed the basis of astrology, a belief that held sway for thousands of years and still has its followers even today.

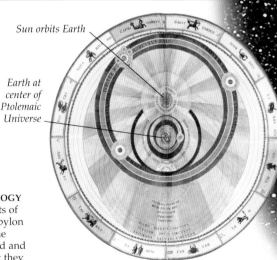

Sun orbits Earth

Earth at center of Ptolemaic Universe

PTOLEMY'S UNIVERSE
The last of the great classical astronomers, an Alexandrian Greek named Ptolemy, summed up the ancient concept of the Universe in about AD 150. The Ptolemaic Universe had the Earth at its center, with the Sun, Moon, and planets circling around it, within a sphere of fixed stars.

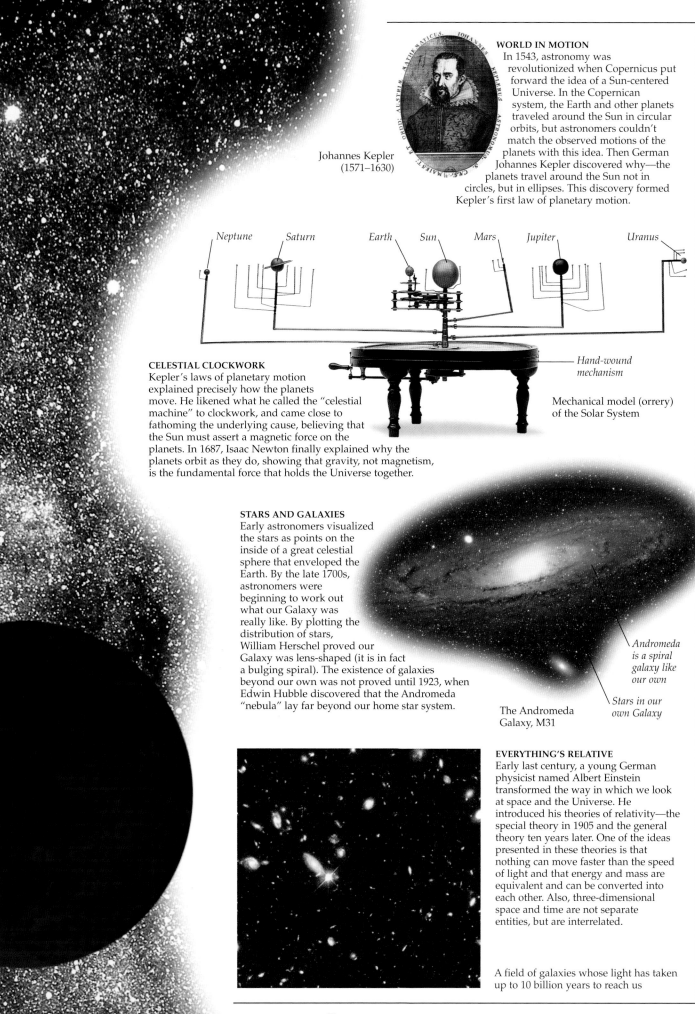

WORLD IN MOTION

In 1543, astronomy was revolutionized when Copernicus put forward the idea of a Sun-centered Universe. In the Copernican system, the Earth and other planets traveled around the Sun in circular orbits, but astronomers couldn't match the observed motions of the planets with this idea. Then German Johannes Kepler discovered why—the planets travel around the Sun not in circles, but in ellipses. This discovery formed Kepler's first law of planetary motion.

Johannes Kepler
(1571–1630)

Neptune   Saturn   Earth   Sun   Mars   Jupiter   Uranus

Hand-wound mechanism

CELESTIAL CLOCKWORK

Kepler's laws of planetary motion explained precisely how the planets move. He likened what he called the "celestial machine" to clockwork, and came close to fathoming the underlying cause, believing that the Sun must assert a magnetic force on the planets. In 1687, Isaac Newton finally explained why the planets orbit as they do, showing that gravity, not magnetism, is the fundamental force that holds the Universe together.

Mechanical model (orrery) of the Solar System

STARS AND GALAXIES

Early astronomers visualized the stars as points on the inside of a great celestial sphere that enveloped the Earth. By the late 1700s, astronomers were beginning to work out what our Galaxy was really like. By plotting the distribution of stars, William Herschel proved our Galaxy was lens-shaped (it is in fact a bulging spiral). The existence of galaxies beyond our own was not proved until 1923, when Edwin Hubble discovered that the Andromeda "nebula" lay far beyond our home star system.

Andromeda is a spiral galaxy like our own

Stars in our own Galaxy

The Andromeda Galaxy, M31

EVERYTHING'S RELATIVE

Early last century, a young German physicist named Albert Einstein transformed the way in which we look at space and the Universe. He introduced his theories of relativity—the special theory in 1905 and the general theory ten years later. One of the ideas presented in these theories is that nothing can move faster than the speed of light and that energy and mass are equivalent and can be converted into each other. Also, three-dimensional space and time are not separate entities, but are interrelated.

A field of galaxies whose light has taken up to 10 billion years to reach us

How do we fit in?

To us earthlings, our planet is the most important thing there is. And not very long ago, people thought our planet was the center of the Universe. But nothing could be farther from the truth—in the Universe as a whole, the Earth is not the least bit special. It is an insignificant speck of rock circling a very ordinary star in an ordinary galaxy in one tiny corner of space. Exactly how big the Universe is, no one really knows. But astronomers are now detecting objects so far away that their light has been traveling toward us for more than 12 billion years. This puts them at a distance of some 70 sextillion miles (120 sextillion kilometers) – a distance beyond our comprehension.

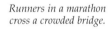

Medieval world map

SMALL COSMOS
In medieval times, before the great voyages of discovery and exploration that began in the 15th century, people assumed that the Earth was the whole Universe. Many supported the idea of a flat Earth—go too far and you would fall over the edge.

SCALE OF THE UNIVERSE
Our insignificance in the Universe as a whole is graphically portrayed in this sequence of images, from life at the human scale to the immeasurable immensity of intergalactic space. One way to help understand the scale of the Universe is to consider how long it would take to travel from place to place, at the speed of light, 186,000 miles per second (300,000 km/s). Astronomers frequently use the light-year (5.9 trillion miles or 9.5 trillion km) as a measure of cosmic distances.

From thousands of miles away, land masses on Earth show up against the blue oceans.

The Oort Cloud of icy, cometlike bodies forms an outer boundary around the whole Solar System. It would take more than six months to reach the Oort Cloud at light speed.

Runners in a marathon cross a crowded bridge.

A satellite in orbit, hundreds of miles above Earth, looks down on the city.

OUR VIEW OF THE UNIVERSE
We look out at the Universe from inside a layer of stars that forms the disk of our Galaxy. We see the greatest density of stars when we look along the plane of this disk— in this direction the Galaxy extends for tens of thousands of light-years. In the night sky, we see this dense band as the Milky Way. To either side of the Milky Way, we are looking out through only a thin layer of stars. By combining satellite images of the sky in all directions, we can capture an overall picture of what the Universe looks like from inside our Galaxy (left).

In the Solar System, the Earth lies three planets out from the Sun. It would take over eight minutes to travel to the Sun at the speed of light.

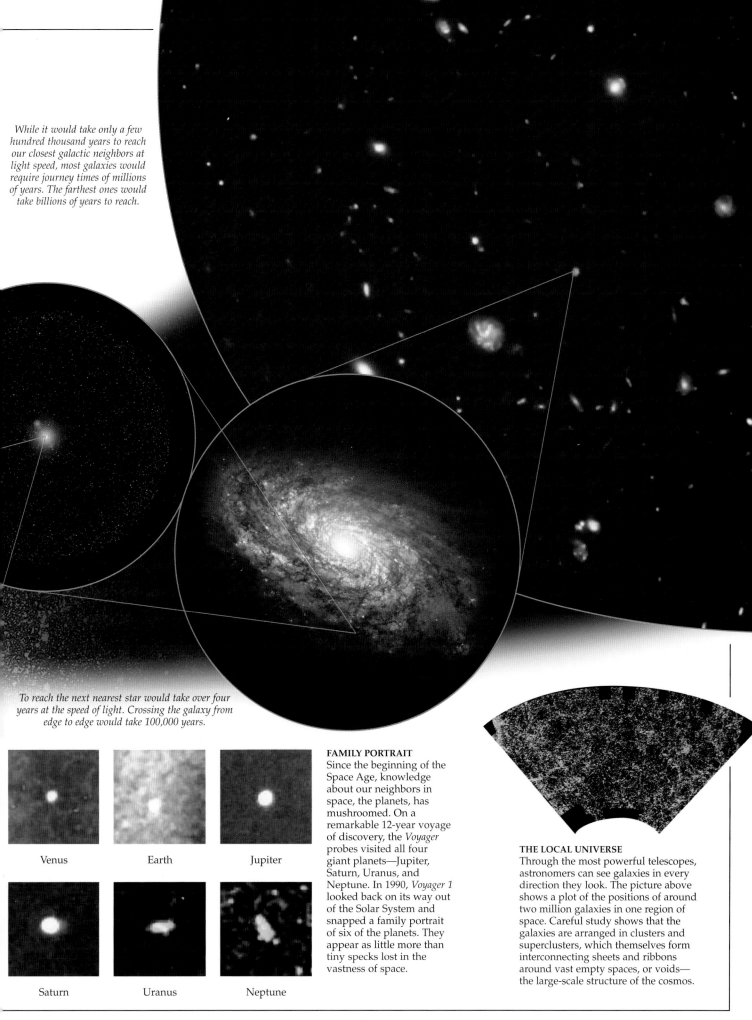

While it would take only a few hundred thousand years to reach our closest galactic neighbors at light speed, most galaxies would require journey times of millions of years. The farthest ones would take billions of years to reach.

To reach the next nearest star would take over four years at the speed of light. Crossing the galaxy from edge to edge would take 100,000 years.

Venus

Earth

Jupiter

Saturn

Uranus

Neptune

FAMILY PORTRAIT
Since the beginning of the Space Age, knowledge about our neighbors in space, the planets, has mushroomed. On a remarkable 12-year voyage of discovery, the *Voyager* probes visited all four giant planets—Jupiter, Saturn, Uranus, and Neptune. In 1990, *Voyager 1* looked back on its way out of the Solar System and snapped a family portrait of six of the planets. They appear as little more than tiny specks lost in the vastness of space.

THE LOCAL UNIVERSE
Through the most powerful telescopes, astronomers can see galaxies in every direction they look. The picture above shows a plot of the positions of around two million galaxies in one region of space. Careful study shows that the galaxies are arranged in clusters and superclusters, which themselves form interconnecting sheets and ribbons around vast empty spaces, or voids— the large-scale structure of the cosmos.

How the Universe works

THE UNIVERSE IS MADE UP of scattered islands of matter in a vast ocean of empty space. Energy travels through the Universe in the form of light and other radiation. Fundamental forces and laws dictate what matter is like and how it behaves. The strongest of the four fundamental forces (the strong force) binds particles together in the nucleus of atoms. The weak and electromagnetic forces also act within the atom. Electromagnetism binds electrons to the nucleus; it also creates the phenomena of electricity and magnetism. Gravity is the weakest of the fundamental forces, but operates over the greatest distances to hold the Universe together.

Water droplet

Water molecule consists of one oxygen and two hydrogen atoms

Protons have a positive electric charge

Inside atom, electrons orbit a tiny nucleus

Neutrons have no charge

Electrons have a negative electric charge

Nucleus

Protons and neutrons are made up of even tinier particles called quarks

INSIDE ATOMS
The atoms that make up matter are not indivisible, as Democritus and Dalton thought. They are made up in turn of tinier, subatomic particles. The three main particles are protons, neutrons, and electrons. The protons and neutrons are found in the center, or nucleus, of an atom, while the electrons circle in orbits around the nucleus.

ELEMENTS AND ATOMS
Greek philosopher Empedocles (c. 490–430 BC) believed matter was made up of four ingredients, or elements—fire, air, water, and earth. His fellow philosopher Democritus (c. 460–370 BC) thought instead that matter was made of tiny, indivisible bits he called atoms. His ideas were forgotten until English chemist John Dalton (1766–1844) laid the foundations of modern atomic theory in 1808. Matter is made of different chemical elements; each is unique because it is made up of different atoms.

Empedocles

Radio waves (wavelengths 1 mm or more)

Peak

Trough

Trough

Wavelength

A FAMILY OF WAVES
The radiation that carries energy through the Universe takes the form of electric and magnetic disturbances that we call electromagnetic waves. There are many kinds of radiation, differing in wavelength—the distance between one peak or trough of the wave and the next. Visible light is radiation that our eyes can detect. It has wavelengths between 390 and 700 nanometers (nm) that we see as colors from violet to red (one nanometer is a billionth of a meter). There are invisible wavelengths shorter than violet light and longer than red. Gamma rays have wavelengths of fractions of a nanometer, while radio waves can be miles long.

Particle tracks at the European nuclear research center in Geneva

Similar poles of magnets repel each other

Iron filings reveal invisible lines of magnetic field

PROBING THE ATOM
Physicists use incredibly powerful machines called particle accelerators, or "atom smashers," to investigate the structure of atoms. These machines accelerate beams of subatomic particles and smash them into atoms or other particle beams. The force of collision generates showers of subatomic particles, which leave trails of tiny bubbles in detectors called bubble chambers.

MAGNETISM
Magnetism is the force that makes magnets attract iron filings. The Earth has magnetism, too. When suspended, a magnet will align itself north–south, in the direction of our planet's magnetic field. Earth's magnetism extends far out into space, creating a bubblelike region called the magnetosphere. Other planets have powerful magnetic fields; so do the Sun and the stars.

GRAVITY

English scientist Isaac Newton (1642–1727) established the basic law of gravity: that every body attracts every other body because of its mass. The more massive a body, the greater its gravitational attraction. With nearly 100 times the mass of Earth, Saturn has enormous gravity. Its pull keeps rings of particles circling around its equator and at least 30 moons in orbit around it. In turn, Saturn is held in the grip of the Sun's gravity, like all the planets. The Sun's gravity reaches out trillions of miles into space.

Saturn, its rings, and two of its satellites photographed by the Hubble Space Telescope

"The most incomprehensible thing about the world is that it is comprehensible."

ALBERT EINSTEIN

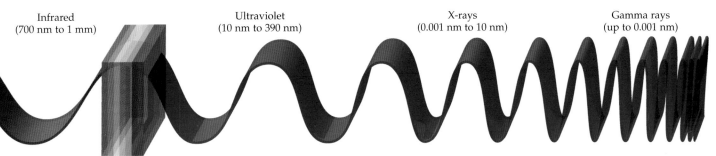

Infrared
(700 nm to 1 mm)

Ultraviolet
(10 nm to 390 nm)

X-rays
(0.001 nm to 10 nm)

Gamma rays
(up to 0.001 nm)

Visible light
(390 nm to 700 nm)

Europe's infrared observatory ISO

ISO view of Rho Ophiuchi star-forming region

THE HIDDEN UNIVERSE

With our eyes, we see the Universe as it appears in visible light. But the Universe gives out radiation at invisible wavelengths as well, from gamma rays to radio waves. We can study radio waves from the heavens with ground-based radio telescopes. Other invisible radiation can only be studied from space, using satellites. If we could see at other wavelengths, the Universe would appear quite different.

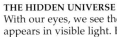

ENERGY AND LIGHT

When you heat up an iron poker in a fire, its color changes, from gray to dull red, to bright red, and to yellow-white. As the temperature rises, the iron gives out shorter wavelengths (colors) of light. It is the same in space—the coolest red stars have a temperature of less than 5,400°F (3,000°C), while the hottest blue-white stars have temperatures more than ten times greater. Even hotter, higher-energy objects emit mostly ultraviolet and X-ray radiation.

In the beginning

WE HAVE A GOOD IDEA of what the Universe is like today and what makes it tick. But where did it come from? How old is it? How has it evolved? What will happen to it in the future? The branch of astronomy that studies and attempts to answer these questions is known as cosmology. Cosmologists think they know when and how the Universe began and has evolved, although they are not so certain about how it might end (see p.14). They believe that an explosive event called the Big Bang, around 12 billion years ago, created the Universe and started it expanding. Amazingly, cosmologists have worked out the history of the Universe since it was one-ten-million-trillion-trillion-trillionth of a second old. It was at this time that the known laws of physics and the fundamental forces of nature came into being.

WHAT CAME BEFORE?
The question "What came before the Big Bang?" has no meaning. Nothing existed before the Big Bang—no matter, no space, no radiation, no laws of physics, no time. There was no "before," only "after." The Big Bang was the beginning of everything. In a similar way, for a newborn baby, there is no "before," only "after."

HOW THE UNIVERSE EVOLVED
The most drastic changes in the Universe occurred in the first three minutes after the Big Bang. During this time, the temperature of the Universe fell from countless trillion trillions of degrees to about a billion degrees. This dramatic cooling allowed the conversion of energy into subatomic particles, such as electrons, and hydrogen and helium nuclei. But it took a further 300,000 years before these particles combined to form atoms of hydrogen and helium, which would later seed the first galaxies.

ABBÉ GEORGES LEMAÎTRE
Around 1930, Georges Lemaître (1894–1966), a Belgian priest turned cosmologist, suggested the Universe was created in a single moment when a "primeval atom" exploded. Matter was scattered into space and eventually condensed into stars and galaxies. Lemaître's ideas laid the foundation for the Big Bang theory.

Big Bang creates the Universe, which is infinitely small, infinitely hot, and full of energy

Energy from the Big Bang creates particles of matter and antimatter, which annihilate one another

As the Universe cools, combinations of particles become stable

A fraction of a second into its life, the Universe expands to an enormous size in an event called inflation

As the Universe cools down, quarks become the dominant type of matter

Quarks collide to form protons and neutrons, the particles found in atomic nuclei

Matter too dense for light to travel freely

Universe expanding from Big Bang

Light waves bounce off particles before traveling far, just as in a fog

Lightweight electrons and positron particles form

Temperature drops through 5,500°F (3,000°C) and electrons are soaked up into atoms

Most electrons and positrons collide and annihilate each other

Temperature is steadily dropping

Matter condenses to form galaxies and clusters

BECOMING TRANSPARENT
Until the Universe was about 300,000 years old, it was full of particles and opaque. Then electrons began combining with atomic nuclei to form the first atoms, an event called decoupling. The fog of particles suddenly cleared, and radiation was able to travel long distances for the first time. The Universe became transparent.

Photons now travel freely in largely empty space

Photons from the time of decoupling are the earliest we can hope to detect

Penzias and Wilson with
their radio horn antenna

Blue areas are
colder and
denser

Red areas
are warmer
and emptier

RIPPLES IN THE COSMOS

For the galaxies we see today to have formed, the Universe must be
"lumpy"—even at the earliest times, matter must have clumped together
in certain areas. The COBE (Cosmic Background Explorer) satellite made
the first accurate map of the radiation left over from the Big Bang (above).
It shows slight variations in the background temperature, which are
believed to reflect the lumpiness in the early Universe.

ECHOES OF THE BIG BANG

If the Big Bang really happened, physicists calculate that
by now the temperature of the whole Universe would
have fallen to about 5.5°F (3°C) above absolute zero,
–459°F (–273°C). In 1965, US physicists Arno Penzias and
Robert Wilson picked up weak radio signals coming from
all parts of the sky. They were equivalent to a cosmic
background temperature of around –454°F (–270°C),
providing convincing evidence for the Big Bang.

BOOMERANG

The joint US/European
BOOMERANG project flies
microwave instruments into
the stratosphere around
Antarctica on balloons.
Ten-day missions are typical,
with the balloon riding the
winds that circle the South
Pole. With its detectors
cooled to a fraction of a
degree above absolute zero,
BOOMERANG can map the
microwave background with
great precision.

A relatively
small number
of electrons
survive

Protons and
neutrons combine to
form atomic nuclei

Electrons still
unattached

Electrons combine
with nuclei to
form atoms

The Universe as it
is today, full of
galaxies, stars, and
planets, and still
expanding

Universe still opaque.
Pressure of radiation
stops most matter from
clumping together.

Universe becomes
transparent

Matter starts
to condense

Fate of the Universe

EINSTEIN'S MISTAKE?
In 1917, when Albert Einstein (1879–1955) set out to describe the Universe mathematically, he included a "cosmological constant"— an outward force to prevent the Universe from collapsing. At the time he did not know that the cosmos is in fact expanding. His "mistaken" idea has recently been revived with the concept of dark energy.

THE BIG BANG CREATED THE UNIVERSE and started it growing, and it has been expanding ever since. But what will happen in the future— what is the fate of the cosmos? Is it an open Universe that will continue to expand forever? Or is it a closed Universe that will one day stop expanding and maybe even shrink? The answer depends on how much matter there is in the Universe. If there is enough, then gravity will one day reign in the galaxies and stop the Universe from expanding. If there is not enough matter, then the Universe will expand forever. There is certainly not enough visible matter in the Universe to stop it from expanding. But there might be enough invisible or dark matter.

UNIVERSAL EXPANSION
From Earth, we find that galaxies are rushing away from us in every direction. They are not just rushing away from us, but also from one another. You can imagine the expansion by thinking of the Universe as being like a balloon, with the galaxies scattered on the surface. With each extra blow into the balloon, the Universe expands, and the galaxies move farther apart.

Galaxies were closer together in the early Universe

Big Bang—origin of the Universe's expansion

Distance between galaxies is increasing

Present-day Universe

Universe a few billion years ago

THE EXPANDING UNIVERSE
In 1917, US astronomer Vesto Slipher found that most galaxies he studied were rushing away from us (see below). The Universe seemed to be expanding. Using the Hooker telescope (above) at Mount Wilson Observatory, Edwin Hubble discovered that the rate of expansion depends on distance. The more distant a galaxy, the faster it is traveling.

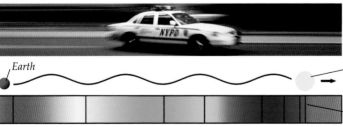

Earth

Star moving away from Earth

Spectral lines formed by elements in star shift to the red

RED SHIFTS
When an emergency vehicle speeds past us, we hear the pitch of its siren drop. The wavelength of sound waves reaching us is stretched as the source moves away and each wave takes longer to reach us. Similarly, light waves from a receding galaxy are stretched to longer (redder) wavelengths. The color change is hard to detect, but the shift is easily measured in changes to the dark "spectral lines."

The Universe does not
have a center, but from
any point within it, all
the distant galaxies seem
to be moving away

FATE OF THE UNIVERSE
If there is enough matter in the Universe, gravity will eventually
stop it from expanding. Maybe it will then contract, with all its
matter pulled together into an infinitely small point. This
"Big Crunch" might then be followed by another Big
Bang to create a new, expanding Universe. But if
there is not enough matter in our
Universe, it will continue to
expand for ever.

New Universe?

Big Crunch

Big Bang

Universe
many billions
of years ago

Universe expands
and cools

Closed Universe
reaches maximum
size

Closed Universe
collapses back on
itself

Open Universe
expands and cools
forever

Galaxy structures
are also evolving
over time

DARK MATTER
As much as 90 percent of
matter in the Universe is
invisible. This dark
matter exists in halos
around galaxies as
MACHOs (massive
compact halo objects),
such as black holes and
brown dwarfs. But most
dark matter is probably
made of WIMPs,
weakly interacting
massive particles.

Gravitational lensing by dark matter

DARK DETECTIVES
As their name suggests, weakly
interacting massive particles (WIMPs)
have some mass but do not interact
with ordinary matter. This makes
them very difficult to detect.
The most elusive of known
particles, neutrinos, may in fact
be WIMPs—until recently they
were thought to be massless, but
new experiments indicate that
they do have a tiny mass. If so,
neutrinos might make up a
significant amount of dark matter.

Tracks of neutrinos in a detector

STRETCHY SPACE
In 1998, astronomers made a
discovery that suggests that the
Universe is open and will expand
forever. They found evidence that
expansion of the Universe is
accelerating. There seems to be
an unknown factor that is
stretching space, which has
been termed dark energy.
It has an effect similar
to Einstein's original
cosmological constant.

Each area of
space expands
slightly

Slight expansions add
up to become visible
over huge distances

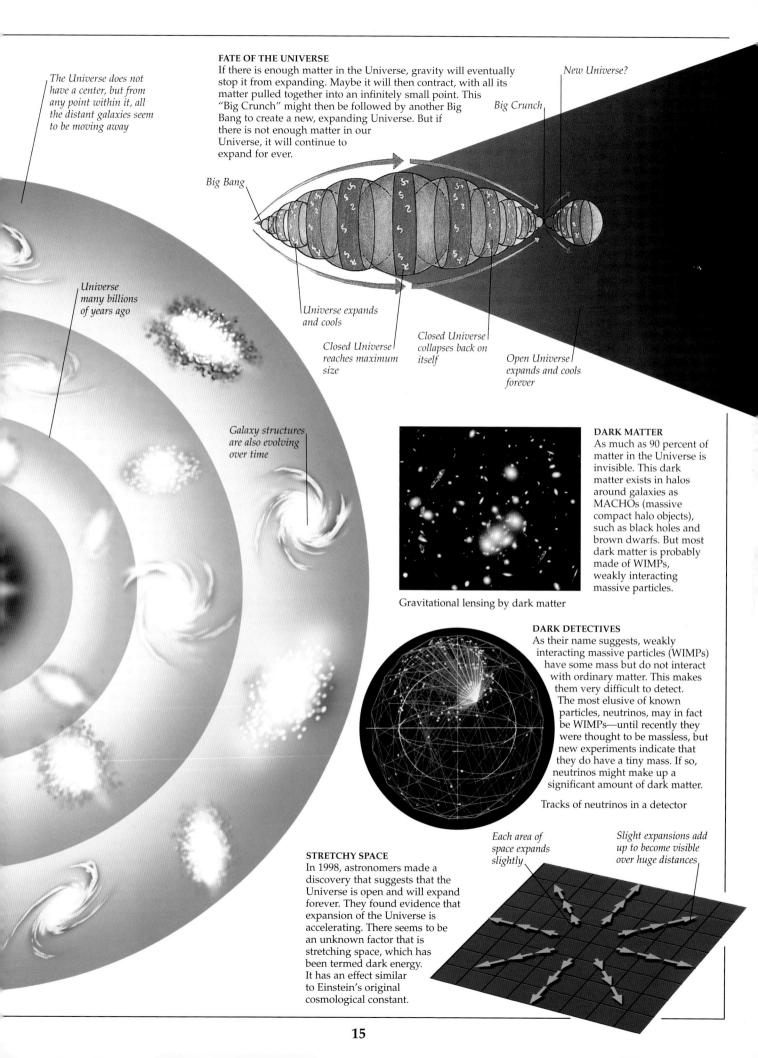

Exploring the Universe

Astronomers have spent more than five millennia gazing at the heavens, studying the stars and constellations, following the Moon through its phases, watching the planets wander through the zodiac, seeing comets come and go, and witnessing eclipses. A giant leap in astronomy came when Galileo first turned a telescope on the heavens in 1609. Since then, ever larger telescopes have revealed ever more secrets of a Universe vaster than anyone can imagine. Other kinds of telescopes have been built to study the invisible radiations stars and galaxies give out. Radio waves can be studied from the ground, but other rays have to be studied from space because the Earth's atmosphere absorbs them as they pass through it.

LOOKING WITH LENSES
Some of the lens-type telescopes, or refractors, used by early astronomers reached an amazing size. They used small light-gathering lenses with a long "focal length" to achieve greater magnification. Christiaan Huygens' giant "aerial telescope" (above) was 210 ft (64 m) long.

Eyepiece

Incoming light rays

Aperture allows light to reach primary mirror

Magnetometer detects Earth's magnetic field

Light rays reflected inward

Primary mirror

Secondary mirror bounces light to eyepiece

NEWTONIAN REFLECTOR
Most astronomical telescopes use mirrors to gather and focus light. Some still follow Isaac Newton's original design from around 1671. A large curved primary mirror gathers and focuses the light, reflecting it back along the telescope tube onto a secondary plane (flat) mirror. This mirror in turn reflects the light into an eyepiece mounted near the front of the tube. In most professional telescopes, the eyepiece is replaced by cameras or other instruments.

Mounting allows accurate pointing of telescope—this is a "Dobsonian" mount

THE HUBBLE SPACE TELESCOPE
The Hubble Space Telescope (HST) is a reflector with a 7.9-ft (2.4-m) mirror. It circles the Earth every 90 minutes in an orbit about 380 miles (610 km) high. It made a disastrous debut in 1990, when its primary mirror was found to be flawed. But its vision was corrected, and the satellite is now sending back the most spectacular images ever taken in space. High above the atmosphere, it views the Universe with perfect clarity, not only at visible wavelengths, but in the ultraviolet and infrared as well.

Solar arrays produce 3,000 watts of electricity

Domes of the Keck Telescopes, Mauna Kea, Hawaii

Comet Wild 2

GOING THERE
Space probes have been winging their way to explore the Moon, planets, and other bodies in the Solar System since 1959. Most fly by their targets; some go into orbit around them; others even land. *Stardust* was designed to encounter Comet Wild 2 in 2004 and return samples of its dust to Earth two years later.

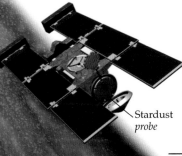

Stardust probe

TWIN KECKS
The two Keck telescopes in Hawaii are among the most powerful in the world. They have light-gathering mirrors measuring 33 ft (10 m) across. These mirrors are made not in one piece, but from 36 separate segments. Each is individually supported and computer controlled so that it always forms, with the others, a perfect mirror shape. When the two telescopes are linked, they can create an effective mirror 280 ft (85 m) in diameter.

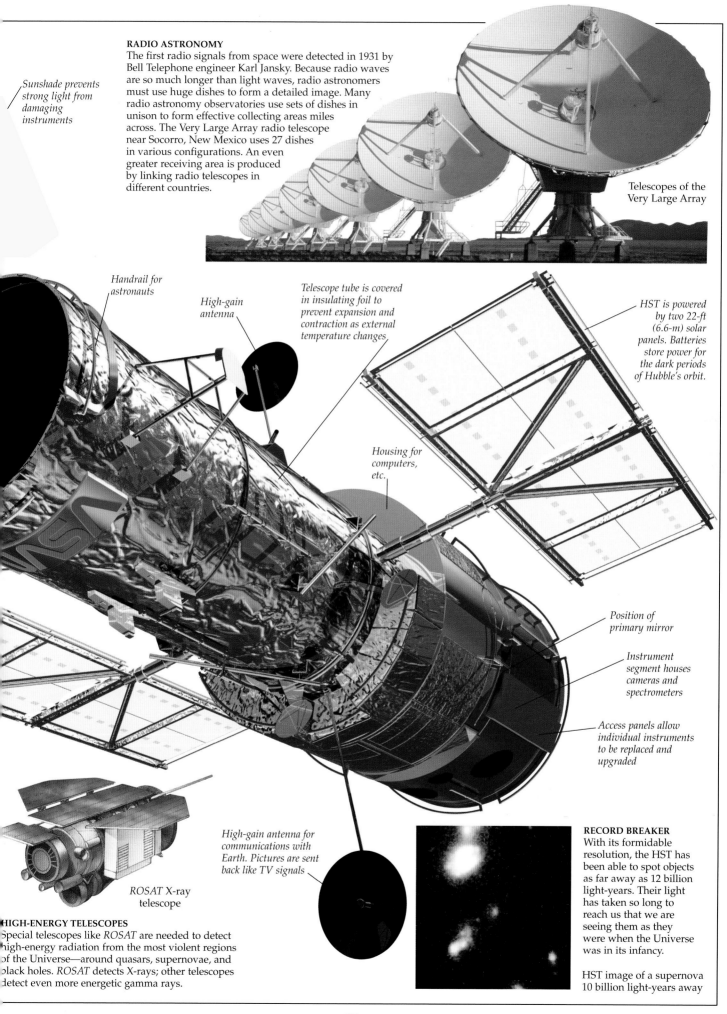

RADIO ASTRONOMY
The first radio signals from space were detected in 1931 by Bell Telephone engineer Karl Jansky. Because radio waves are so much longer than light waves, radio astronomers must use huge dishes to form a detailed image. Many radio astronomy observatories use sets of dishes in unison to form effective collecting areas miles across. The Very Large Array radio telescope near Socorro, New Mexico uses 27 dishes in various configurations. An even greater receiving area is produced by linking radio telescopes in different countries.

Sunshade prevents strong light from damaging instruments

Telescopes of the Very Large Array

Handrail for astronauts

High-gain antenna

Telescope tube is covered in insulating foil to prevent expansion and contraction as external temperature changes

HST is powered by two 22-ft (6.6-m) solar panels. Batteries store power for the dark periods of Hubble's orbit.

Housing for computers, etc.

Position of primary mirror

Instrument segment houses cameras and spectrometers

Access panels allow individual instruments to be replaced and upgraded

High-gain antenna for communications with Earth. Pictures are sent back like TV signals

ROSAT X-ray telescope

HIGH-ENERGY TELESCOPES
Special telescopes like *ROSAT* are needed to detect high-energy radiation from the most violent regions of the Universe—around quasars, supernovae, and black holes. *ROSAT* detects X-rays; other telescopes detect even more energetic gamma rays.

RECORD BREAKER
With its formidable resolution, the HST has been able to spot objects as far away as 12 billion light-years. Their light has taken so long to reach us that we are seeing them as they were when the Universe was in its infancy.

HST image of a supernova 10 billion light-years away

Our corner of the Universe

ANCIENT ASTRONOMERS BELIEVED that Earth had to be the center of the Universe. Didn't the Sun, the Moon, and all the other heavenly bodies and the stars revolve around it? Of course, today we know they don't—the Sun is really the center of our little corner of the Universe, and the Earth and planets circle around that body. They are part of the Sun's family, or Solar System. The Sun is different from all other bodies in the Solar System because it is a star, and it is the only body that produces light of its own. We see all the other objects by the sunlight they reflect. Nine planets, including Earth, are the most important members of the Solar System, along with dozens of moons. The billions of minor members include rocky lumps called asteroids and icy bodies called comets.

THE COPERNICAN SYSTEM
In 1543, Polish astronomer and priest Nicolaus Copernicus (1473–1543) put our corner of the Universe in order, suggesting that the Sun and not the Earth was at the center of our planetary system. The idea contradicted the teachings of the Church, but was eventually proved by Galileo.

PLANETS
A planet is a world that orbits the Sun and is big enough to pull itself into a roughly spherical shape through its own gravity. Our planet, Earth, is the third from the Sun, and its position provides perfect conditions for life.

MOONS
All the planets except Mercury and Venus have satellites, or moons, circling around them. The four giant outer planets have more than 80 moons between them. This is Saturn's moon Mimas.

Mercury

Orbit of Neptune. Neptune takes 165 years to orbit the Sun

Mars takes 1.9 years to orbit the Sun

Mars

Pluto

Pluto's orbit is highly elongated. It takes 248 years to orbit the Sun once, and sometimes comes closer to the Sun than Neptune.

Jupiter takes 12 years to orbit the Sun

Jupiter

The Asteroid Belt contains thousands of rocky lumps

Uranus

Small icy worlds called Centaurs orbit close to Saturn and Uranus

Saturn takes 30 years to orbit the Sun

Uranus takes 84 years to orbit the Sun

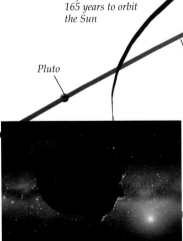

KUIPER BELT OBJECTS
Many icy bodies similar to Pluto exist in the outer Solar System. They are found in a region known as the Kuiper Belt after astronomer Gerard Kuiper. The belt is the source of many comets.

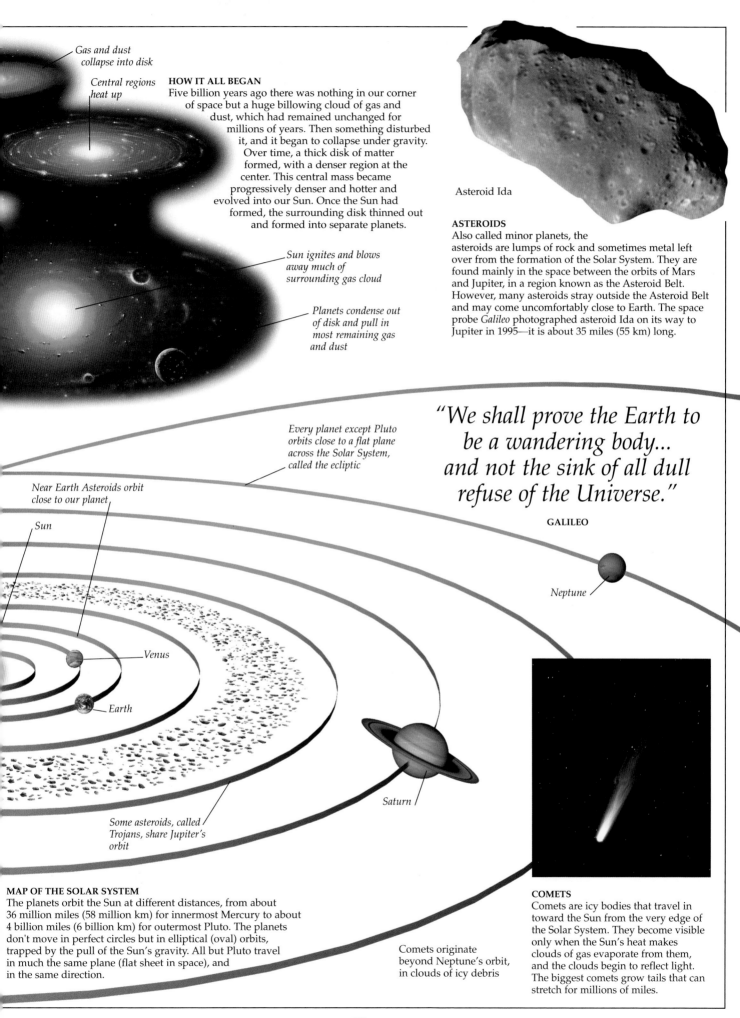

Gas and dust collapse into disk

Central regions heat up

HOW IT ALL BEGAN

Five billion years ago there was nothing in our corner of space but a huge billowing cloud of gas and dust, which had remained unchanged for millions of years. Then something disturbed it, and it began to collapse under gravity. Over time, a thick disk of matter formed, with a denser region at the center. This central mass became progressively denser and hotter and evolved into our Sun. Once the Sun had formed, the surrounding disk thinned out and formed into separate planets.

Sun ignites and blows away much of surrounding gas cloud

Planets condense out of disk and pull in most remaining gas and dust

Asteroid Ida

ASTEROIDS

Also called minor planets, the asteroids are lumps of rock and sometimes metal left over from the formation of the Solar System. They are found mainly in the space between the orbits of Mars and Jupiter, in a region known as the Asteroid Belt. However, many asteroids stray outside the Asteroid Belt and may come uncomfortably close to Earth. The space probe *Galileo* photographed asteroid Ida on its way to Jupiter in 1995—it is about 35 miles (55 km) long.

Every planet except Pluto orbits close to a flat plane across the Solar System, called the ecliptic

"We shall prove the Earth to be a wandering body... and not the sink of all dull refuse of the Universe."

GALILEO

Near Earth Asteroids orbit close to our planet

Sun

Neptune

Venus

Earth

Saturn

Some asteroids, called Trojans, share Jupiter's orbit

MAP OF THE SOLAR SYSTEM

The planets orbit the Sun at different distances, from about 36 million miles (58 million km) for innermost Mercury to about 4 billion miles (6 billion km) for outermost Pluto. The planets don't move in perfect circles but in elliptical (oval) orbits, trapped by the pull of the Sun's gravity. All but Pluto travel in much the same plane (flat sheet in space), and in the same direction.

Comets originate beyond Neptune's orbit, in clouds of icy debris

COMETS

Comets are icy bodies that travel in toward the Sun from the very edge of the Solar System. They become visible only when the Sun's heat makes clouds of gas evaporate from them, and the clouds begin to reflect light. The biggest comets grow tails that can stretch for millions of miles.

Our local star

THE STAR WE CALL THE SUN dominates our corner of space. With a diameter of about 870,000 miles (1,400,000 km), it is more than a hundred times wider than the Earth. Because of its huge mass, it has powerful gravity and attracts a vast collection of objects, both large (such as the Earth and the other planets) and small (such as comets). These bodies form the Sun's family, or Solar System. Like other stars, the Sun is a giant ball of incandescent gas, or rather, gases. The two main ones are hydrogen and helium, but there are small amounts of up to 70 other chemical elements as well. To us on Earth, 93 million miles (150 million kilometers) away, the Sun is all-important. It provides the light and warmth needed to make our planet suitable for life.

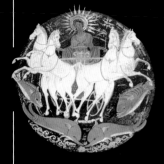

SUN LEGENDS
The Sun was worshipped as a god from the earliest times. In ancient Egypt, the falcon-headed sun god Re was the most powerful deity. In early Greek mythology, the sun god Helios carried the Sun across the heavens every day in a horse-drawn flying chariot.

Visible surface of the Sun is called the photosphere

Prominences are fountains of hot gas that loop above the surface

The Sun's visible surface is made up of fine "granulations"

Photosphere's temperature is around 9,000°F (5,500°C)

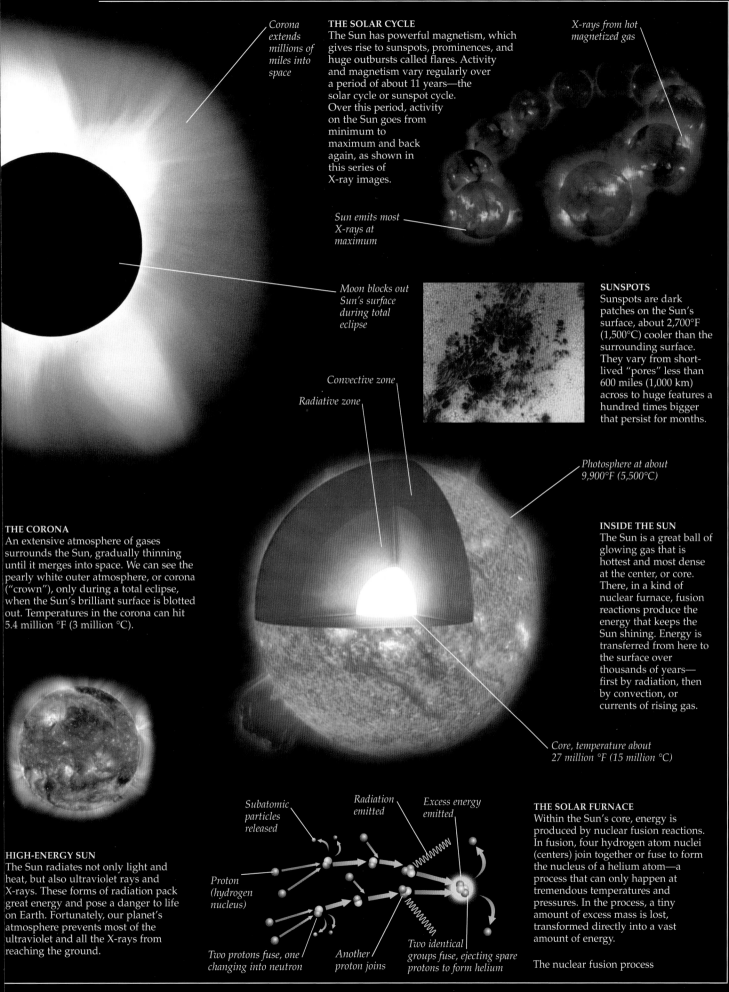

Corona extends millions of miles into space

THE SOLAR CYCLE
The Sun has powerful magnetism, which gives rise to sunspots, prominences, and huge outbursts called flares. Activity and magnetism vary regularly over a period of about 11 years—the solar cycle or sunspot cycle. Over this period, activity on the Sun goes from minimum to maximum and back again, as shown in this series of X-ray images.

X-rays from hot magnetized gas

Sun emits most X-rays at maximum

Moon blocks out Sun's surface during total eclipse

Convective zone

Radiative zone

SUNSPOTS
Sunspots are dark patches on the Sun's surface, about 2,700°F (1,500°C) cooler than the surrounding surface. They vary from short-lived "pores" less than 600 miles (1,000 km) across to huge features a hundred times bigger that persist for months.

Photosphere at about 9,900°F (5,500°C)

THE CORONA
An extensive atmosphere of gases surrounds the Sun, gradually thinning until it merges into space. We can see the pearly white outer atmosphere, or corona ("crown"), only during a total eclipse, when the Sun's brilliant surface is blotted out. Temperatures in the corona can hit 5.4 million °F (3 million °C).

INSIDE THE SUN
The Sun is a great ball of glowing gas that is hottest and most dense at the center, or core. There, in a kind of nuclear furnace, fusion reactions produce the energy that keeps the Sun shining. Energy is transferred from here to the surface over thousands of years—first by radiation, then by convection, or currents of rising gas.

Core, temperature about 27 million °F (15 million °C)

Subatomic particles released

Radiation emitted

Excess energy emitted

HIGH-ENERGY SUN
The Sun radiates not only light and heat, but also ultraviolet rays and X-rays. These forms of radiation pack great energy and pose a danger to life on Earth. Fortunately, our planet's atmosphere prevents most of the ultraviolet and all the X-rays from reaching the ground.

Proton (hydrogen nucleus)

Two protons fuse, one changing into neutron

Another proton joins

Two identical groups fuse, ejecting spare protons to form helium

THE SOLAR FURNACE
Within the Sun's core, energy is produced by nuclear fusion reactions. In fusion, four hydrogen atom nuclei (centers) join together or fuse to form the nucleus of a helium atom—a process that can only happen at tremendous temperatures and pressures. In the process, a tiny amount of excess mass is lost, transformed directly into a vast amount of energy.

The nuclear fusion process

Earth's Moon

THE MOON IS EARTH'S CLOSEST companion in space, its only natural satellite. On average, it lies 239,000 miles (384,000 km) away. It has no light of its own, but shines by reflected sunlight. As the Moon circles the Earth every month, it appears to change shape, from slim crescent to full circle and back again every 29.5 days. We call these changing shapes the phases of the moon, and they mark one of the great rhythms of nature. With a diameter of 2,160 miles (3,476 km), the Moon is a rocky world like the Earth, but has no atmosphere, water, or life. Astronomers think that the Moon was formed from the debris flung into space in a collision between Earth and another large body many eons ago.

Bright crater surrounded by rays

Craters formed when meteorites crashed into the Moon

New Moon

Crescent

First quarter

Waxing gibbous

Full moon

Waning gibbous

Last quarter

Decrescent

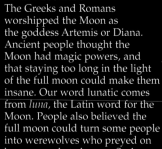

Actor Lon Chaney Jr. in *The Wolf Man* (1941)

LUNAR LEGENDS

The Greeks and Romans worshipped the Moon as the goddess Artemis or Diana. Ancient people thought the Moon had magic powers, and that staying too long in the light of the full moon could make them insane. Our word lunatic comes from *luna*, the Latin word for the Moon. People also believed the full moon could turn some people into werewolves who preyed on humans and ate human flesh.

THE CHANGING FACE

The changing phases of the moon happen as the Sun lights up different amounts of the side that faces Earth. At new moon we can't see the Moon at all because the Sun is lighting up only the far side. As the Moon moves farther around in its orbit, more and more of its face gets lit up until all of it is illuminated at full moon. Then the sunlit side moves on and the Moon's phase decreases, until it disappears completely.

The dark part of the crescent moon sometimes dimly reflects light from Earth

LUNAR GRAVITY

The Moon's gravity is only about one-sixth of Earth's, so it has been unable to hang onto any gases to make an atmosphere. The lack of atmosphere means the temperature varies widely from day (around 230°F, 110°C) to night (around –290°F, –180°C). Weak though it is, the Moon's gravity still affects the Earth. It tugs at the oceans to create tides. The water bulges to form a high tide directly beneath the Moon and also forms a bulge on the opposite side of Earth. On either side of high tide is a low tide where water has been drawn away. There are two highs and two lows roughly every day.

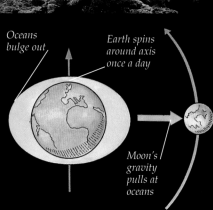

Oceans bulge out

Earth spins around axis once a day

Moon's gravity pulls at oceans

THE FACE OF THE MOON

The Moon always presents the same face toward Earth. This happens because it spins once on its axis in exactly the same time as it circles once around the Earth—27.3 days. This motion is called captured rotation and most moons do it. The dark regions we see on the Moon's face are vast dusty plains. Early astronomers thought they might be seas and called them *maria*, which is Latin for "seas." The brighter regions are much older highlands, which are heavily cratered and are thought to be part of the Moon's original crust.

Aitken Basin is the largest crater in the Solar System

The Moon's south polar region

THE HIDDEN POLES

We never see the Moon's poles from Earth, but space probes have inspected them. They show that some polar craters and basins are in perpetual darkness and could contain large deposits of ice. If proven, these ice deposits could provide water for future human explorers.

WALKING ON THE MOON

On July 20, 1969, *Apollo 11* astronauts Neil Armstrong and Buzz Aldrin planted the first human footprints on the Moon. They were the first of 12 US astronauts who explored "seas" and highland areas, set up scientific stations, and brought back samples of soil and rock. They found that lunar soil, called regolith, is somewhat like plowed-up soil on Earth—it has been crushed by constant bombardment from space. All the rocks are volcanic, often like Earth rocks called basalts.

THE FAR SIDE

No one had seen the far side of the Moon until orbiting probes mapped it in the 1960s. It is much more rugged and heavily cratered than the nearside, and has no large "seas." One of its most prominent features is the 115-mile (185-km) crater Tsiolkovsky.

Dark maria (seas) are frozen lava flows

Lunar highlands

Seen from the Moon, Earth goes through phases

Lunar surface many miles below

EARTHRISE

The *Apollo* astronauts took stunning photographs of the Moon on the surface and also from orbit. None are more dramatic than the shots showing the Earth rising over the Moon's horizon. They show the huge contrast between our colorful, living world and its drab, dead satellite.

Comparing the planets

GOING OUT FROM THE SUN, the nine planets are
Mercury, Venus, Earth, Mars, Jupiter, Saturn, Uranus,
Neptune, and Pluto. They are all different from one
another, but divide mainly into two kinds, depending on
their composition. The four small inner planets are made
up mainly of rock, and the four giant outer ones are
made up mainly of gas. The outermost planet, Pluto,
however, is in a class by itself. It seems to be the largest
of a swarm of icy bodies that populate the outer
Solar System. All the planets have two motions
in space: the period in which a planet spins
on its axis is its "day," and the time it takes
to orbit the Sun is its "year."

THE PLANETS TO SCALE
The planets vary widely in size. Jupiter is truly
gigantic, containing more matter than all the other
planets put together. It could swallow more than
1,300 bodies the size of Earth and over two million
worlds the size of Pluto. Yet the cores at the centers
of the giant planets are much smaller—around
the size of Earth. At the other extreme, Mercury and
Pluto are tiny—the gas giants have some moons
bigger than the first and last planets.

MERCURY
Diameter: 3,032 miles
Distance from Sun:
36 million miles
Rotation period: 58.7 days
Time to orbit Sun: 88 days
Number of moons: 0

EARTH
Diameter: 7,926 miles
Distance from Sun:
93 million miles
Rotation period: 23.93 hours
Time to orbit Sun: 365.25 days
Number of moons: 1

VENUS
Diameter: 7,521 miles
Distance from Sun:
67 million miles
Rotation period: 243 days
Time to orbit Sun: 224.7 days
Number of moons: 0

MARS
Diameter: 4,222 miles
Distance from Sun:
142 million miles
Rotation period: 24.6 hours
Time to orbit Sun: 687 days
Number of moons: 2

*Most gas giants have
turbulent atmospheres
powered by an internal
energy source*

JUPITER
Diameter: 88,846 miles
Distance from Sun:
483.5 million miles
Rotation period: 9.93 hours
Time to orbit Sun: 11.9 years
Number of moons: 39

ORBITS TO SCALE
The diagram across the bottom of this
page shows the distances of the planets
from the Sun to scale. The four inner
planets lie relatively close together, while
the five outer planets lie very far apart. The
Solar System consists mainly of empty space.

*An extensive system of rings surrounds
Saturn's equator, spanning a distance of
some 171,000 miles (275,000 km). All
four gas giants have ring systems, but
Saturn's rings are by far the
most impressive.*

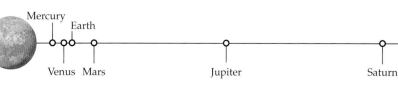

Mercury

Earth

Venus Mars

Jupiter

Saturn

Uran

IN THE ECLIPTIC
The planets circle the Sun close to a flat plane called the plane of the ecliptic. In the Earth's skies, the ecliptic is the path the Sun appears to take through the heavens during a year. From Earth, the planets appear to travel close to this plane, through the constellations of the Zodiac. Dust around the ecliptic causes a faint glow in the night sky called the zodiacal light.

The five naked-eye planets aligned along the ecliptic

As shown by the tilt of Saturn's rings, planets do not orbit the Sun bolt upright—most are tilted over to some extent.

SATURN
Diameter: 74,900 miles
Distance from Sun:
887 million miles
Rotation period: 10.66 hours
Time to orbit Sun: 29.5 years
Number of moons: 30

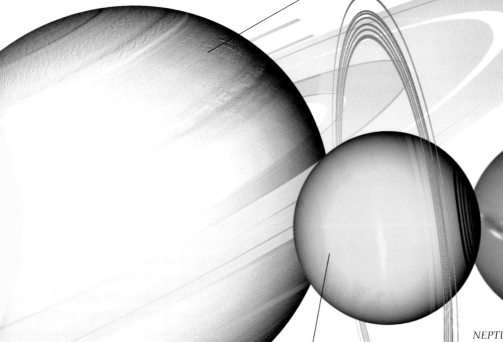

URANUS
Diameter: 31,770 miles
Distance from Sun:
1.79 billion miles
Rotation period: 17.24 hours
Time to orbit Sun: 84 years
Number of moons: 22

NEPTUNE
Diameter: 30,780 miles
Distance from Sun:
2.8 billion miles
Rotation period:
16.11 hours
Time to orbit Sun:
164.8 years
Number of moons: 8

PLUTO
Diameter: 1,413 miles
Distance from Sun:
3.7 billion miles average
Rotation period:
6.39 days
Time to orbit Sun:
247.7 years
Number of moons: 1

Outer atmosphere

Liquid hydrogen molecules

GAS GIANTS
The four planets from Jupiter to Neptune are gas giants. They have a deep atmosphere of mostly hydrogen and helium. Underneath the atmosphere is a planetwide ocean of liquid hydrogen in Jupiter and Saturn, or of slushy ices in the smaller giants. Only at the center is there a small core of rock. The gas giants have two other things in common: they have many moons circling around them, and they have systems of rings.

Structure of Jupiter

Liquid atomic hydrogen

Core

Mantle   *Core*

Crust

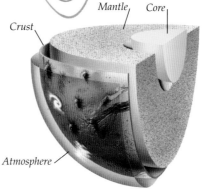

Atmosphere

Structure of Mars

ROCKY PLANETS
The four inner planets, from Mercury to Mars, have a similar, rocky structure. They are known as the terrestrial or Earth-like planets. They have a thin, hard outer layer, or crust, which overlays another thicker layer called the mantle. In the center is a core of metal, mainly iron. All the planets except Mercury have an atmosphere.

Neptune

Pluto

Mercury and Venus

TWO ROCKY PLANETS, Mercury and Venus, orbit closer to the Sun than Earth. We see them shining in the night sky like bright stars. Venus is by far the brightest, shining prominently for much of the year as the evening star. Mercury lies so close to the Sun that it is only visible briefly at certain times of year, just before sunrise or just after sunset. Both planets are much hotter than Earth—surface temperatures on Mercury can rise as high as 840°F (450°C), and on Venus up to 55°F (30°C) higher. But the two planets are very different. Mercury is less than half as big across as Venus, is almost completely covered in craters, and has no appreciable atmosphere. Venus has a very dense atmosphere, full of clouds, which stops us from seeing the surface underneath.

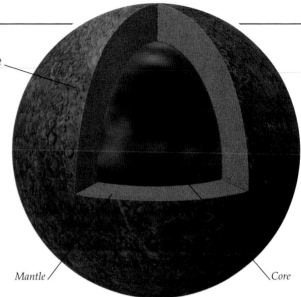

Crust

Mantle

Core

INSIDE MERCURY
Mercury is a small planet, with a diameter of 3,032 miles (4,880 km). It is rocky like Earth and has a similar layered structure. Underneath a hard outer layer, or crust, it has a rocky mantle, then a core of iron. The core is unusually large, extending three-quarters of the way to the surface.

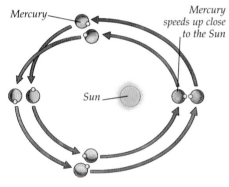

Mercury

Mercury speeds up close to the Sun

Sun

SPEEDY ORBIT
Mercury is the fastest-moving planet, orbiting the Sun in just 88 days. But it rotates very slowly, just once every 59 days. As a result, most parts of the surface spend 176 Earth days in sunlight, followed by an equal time in the dark (shown by the dot in the diagram). Temperatures vary from 840°F (450°C) in daytime to –290°F (–180°C) at night.

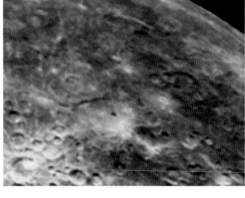

THE CRATERED SURFACE
Mercury was heavily bombarded with meteorites billions of years ago, resulting in the heavily cratered, Moonlike landscape we see today. There are some smoother plains here and there, but nothing like the Moon's seas. The biggest feature is the huge Caloris Basin, an impact crater about 800 miles (1,300 km) across.

Clouds of sulfuric acid

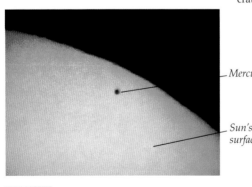

Mercury

Sun's surface

TRANSITS
Mercury and Venus circle the Sun inside the Earth's orbit and can sometimes pass in front of the Sun as seen from Earth. We call these crossings transits. They are rare because the Earth, the planets, and the Sun only very occasionally line up precisely in space. Transits of Venus are rarest, coming in pairs every century or so.

COOK'S TOUR
In 1768, Britain's Royal Society appointed James Cook to command the first scientific expedition to the Pacific Ocean. One of the expedition's prime goals was to record the transit of Venus from Tahiti on June 3, 1769, which could be used to measure the distance from the Earth to the Sun. After making these measurements, Cook sailed his ship *Endeavour* to New Zealand and Australia, where in 1770 he landed at Botany Bay. He claimed the land for Britain and named it New South Wales.

Earth's deadly twin

With a diameter of 7,521 miles (12,104 km), Venus is a near twin of Earth in size. But it is a very different world—its very high temperature and crushing atmosphere make it a most hostile planet. Also, its clouds are made up of droplets of sulfuric acid. If you went to Venus, you would simultaneously be burned, crushed, and roasted to death—and suffocated too, because the atmosphere is nearly all carbon dioxide.

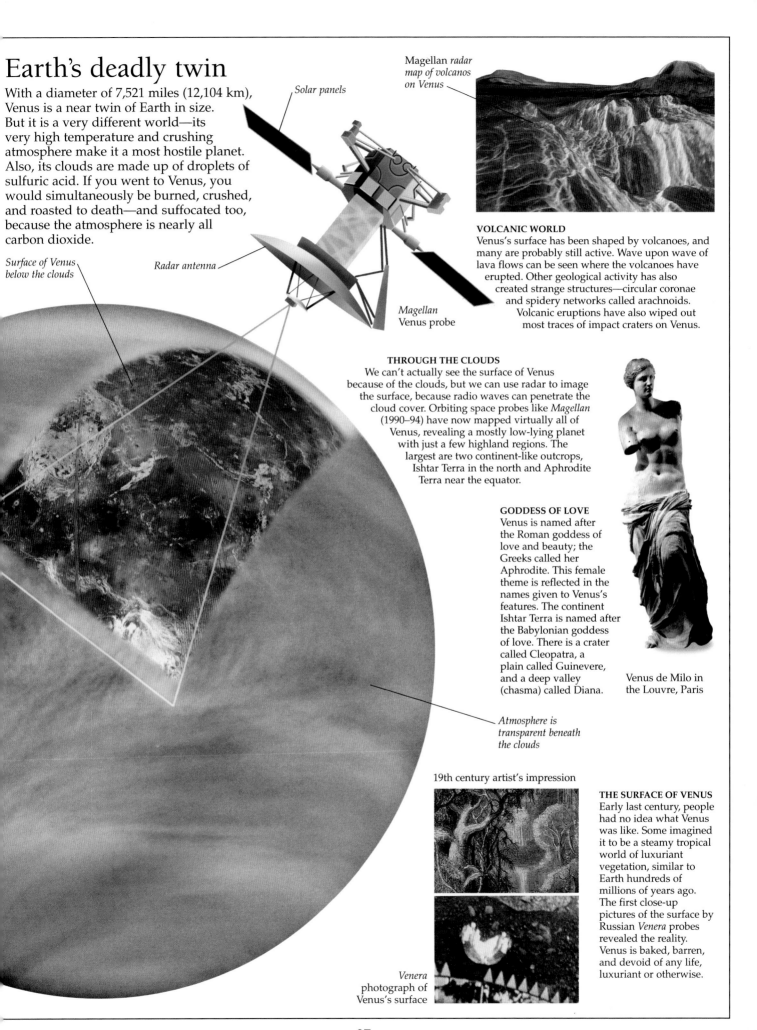

Solar panels

Surface of Venus below the clouds

Radar antenna

Magellan Venus probe

Magellan radar map of volcanos on Venus

VOLCANIC WORLD
Venus's surface has been shaped by volcanoes, and many are probably still active. Wave upon wave of lava flows can be seen where the volcanoes have erupted. Other geological activity has also created strange structures—circular coronae and spidery networks called arachnoids. Volcanic eruptions have also wiped out most traces of impact craters on Venus.

THROUGH THE CLOUDS
We can't actually see the surface of Venus because of the clouds, but we can use radar to image the surface, because radio waves can penetrate the cloud cover. Orbiting space probes like *Magellan* (1990–94) have now mapped virtually all of Venus, revealing a mostly low-lying planet with just a few highland regions. The largest are two continent-like outcrops, Ishtar Terra in the north and Aphrodite Terra near the equator.

GODDESS OF LOVE
Venus is named after the Roman goddess of love and beauty; the Greeks called her Aphrodite. This female theme is reflected in the names given to Venus's features. The continent Ishtar Terra is named after the Babylonian goddess of love. There is a crater called Cleopatra, a plain called Guinevere, and a deep valley (chasma) called Diana.

Venus de Milo in the Louvre, Paris

Atmosphere is transparent beneath the clouds

19th century artist's impression

THE SURFACE OF VENUS
Early last century, people had no idea what Venus was like. Some imagined it to be a steamy tropical world of luxuriant vegetation, similar to Earth hundreds of millions of years ago. The first close-up pictures of the surface by Russian *Venera* probes revealed the reality. Venus is baked, barren, and devoid of any life, luxuriant or otherwise.

Venera photograph of Venus's surface

Home planet

WITH A DIAMETER of 7,926 miles (12,756 km) at the equator, Earth is Venus's near-twin in size, but the similarity ends there. At an average distance of 93 million miles (150 million km) from the Sun, Earth is not a hellish place like Venus, but a comfortable world that is a haven for all kinds of life. It is a rocky planet like the other three inner planets of the Solar System, but is the only one whose surface is not solid—instead, it is broken up into a number of sections, called plates. The plates move slowly over the surface, causing the continents to drift and the oceans to widen.

EARTH GOD
The ancient Egyptian concept of the world is encapsulated in this drawing copied from an ancient papyrus. The Earth god Geb reclines on the ground. His sister, Nut, the star-spangled sky goddess, is held aloft by Shu, a kind of Egyptian Atlas.

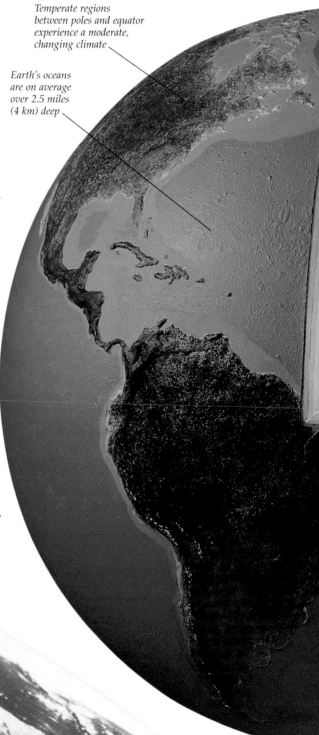

Temperate regions between poles and equator experience a moderate, changing climate

Earth's oceans are on average over 2.5 miles (4 km) deep

PLATE TECTONICS
The study of the Earth's shifting crust is known as plate tectonics. At plate boundaries, colliding plates may destroy rocks and create volcanoes. Here, at the San Andreas fault in California, plates grind past each other and cause earthquakes.

INSIDE THE EARTH
The Earth has a layered structure, rather like an onion. It has an outer layer, or crust, of hard rock. This is very thin, averaging about 25 miles (40 km) on the continents but only about 6 miles (10 km) under the oceans. The crust overlays a heavier rocky mantle, the top part of which is relatively soft and can flow. Deeper down lies a huge iron core. The outer core is liquid, while the inner core is solid. Currents and eddies in the liquid outer core are believed to give rise to the Earth's magnetism.

OCEANS AND ATMOSPHERE
Oceans cover more than 70 percent of Earth's surface. The evaporation of ocean water into the atmosphere plays a crucial role in the planet's climate. This never-ending exchange of moisture between the surface and atmosphere dictates weather patterns around the globe. Most of Earth's weather takes place in the troposphere, the lowest layer of atmosphere, up to about 10 miles (16 km) high.

Earth seen from orbit

Ice caps cover North and South poles

Arid desert regions lie close to the equator

Crust of silicate minerals floats on molten interior

Earth bulges at the equator—its diameter here is 13 miles (21km) more than at the poles

Inner core of solid iron

Outer core of molten iron and nickel

Core may contain a small dense "kernel" at its very center

Outer mantle

Inner mantle richer in iron than outer mantle

Although shown upright, Earth's poles are in fact tilted 23.5° from vertical. As Earth orbits the Sun, one pole and then the other gets more sunlight, creating the seasons.

Antarctica

Death Valley, California

CLIMATE EXTREMES

Antarctica experiences the coldest temperatures on Earth, with a low of −128.6°F (−89.2°C) recorded at Vostok Station in 1983. Death Valley in California is one of the world's hottest places, where temperatures regularly nudge 122°F (50°C) in summer.

THE MAGNETIC SHIELD

Earth's magnetism extends into space, creating a bubblelike cocoon around our planet called the magnetosphere. It acts as a shield against deadly radiation and particles streaming out from the Sun. However, particles trapped in the magnetosphere are often shaken out over the poles. As they interact with the upper atmosphere, they create the beautiful light displays we call the aurorae or northern and southern lights.

Aurorae photographed from the Space Shuttle

LIFE IN ABUNDANCE

With comfortable temperatures, liquid water, and oxygen in the atmosphere, Earth can support an amazing variety of life. This can vary from primitive microscopic organisms like viruses and bacteria to towering redwood trees and a multitude of flowering plants; from creepy-crawly creatures like slugs and spiders to warm-blooded birds and intelligent mammals, like ourselves.

Life thriving on and around a coral reef

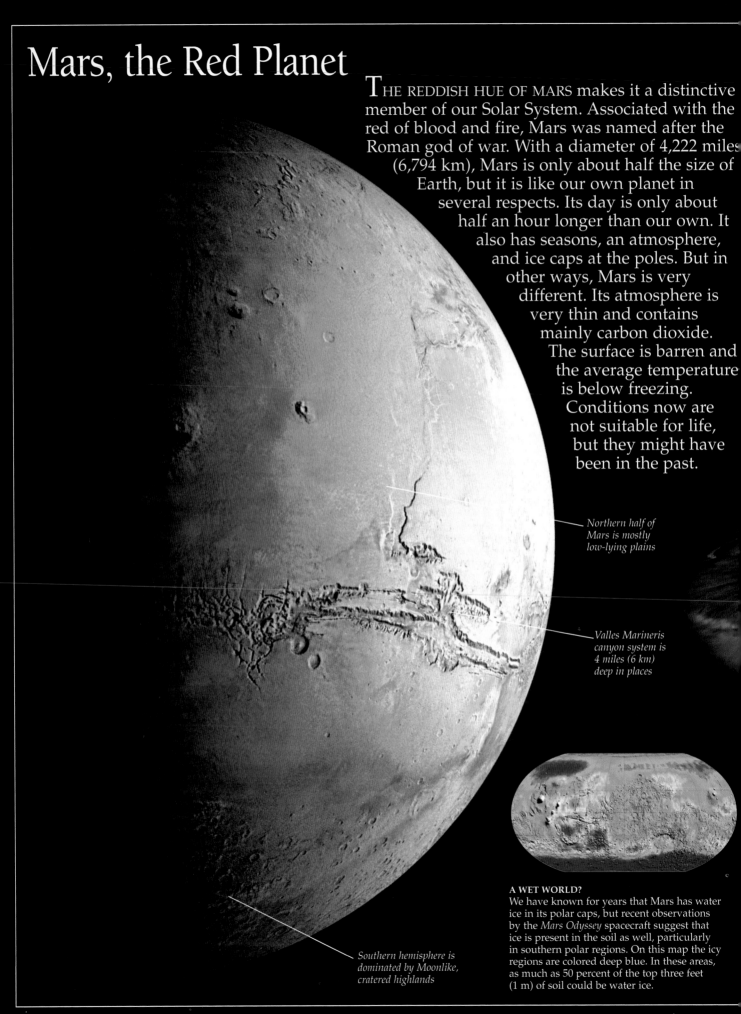

Mars, the Red Planet

THE REDDISH HUE OF MARS makes it a distinctive member of our Solar System. Associated with the red of blood and fire, Mars was named after the Roman god of war. With a diameter of 4,222 miles (6,794 km), Mars is only about half the size of Earth, but it is like our own planet in several respects. Its day is only about half an hour longer than our own. It also has seasons, an atmosphere, and ice caps at the poles. But in other ways, Mars is very different. Its atmosphere is very thin and contains mainly carbon dioxide. The surface is barren and the average temperature is below freezing. Conditions now are not suitable for life, but they might have been in the past.

Northern half of Mars is mostly low-lying plains

Valles Marineris canyon system is 4 miles (6 km) deep in places

Southern hemisphere is dominated by Moonlike, cratered highlands

A WET WORLD?
We have known for years that Mars has water ice in its polar caps, but recent observations by the *Mars Odyssey* spacecraft suggest that ice is present in the soil as well, particularly in southern polar regions. On this map the icy regions are colored deep blue. In these areas, as much as 50 percent of the top three feet (1 m) of soil could be water ice.

EXPLORING THE SURFACE
The surface of Mars has been more extensively explored than that of any other planet. Landing probes like the two *Vikings* (1976) and *Mars Pathfinder* (1997) have taken close-up pictures of the surface. The pictures show rust-colored rocks strewn over a sandy surface. *Pathfinder*'s tiny rover, *Sojourner*, was equipped to analyze the composition of Martian rocks. Most are volcanic, but some seem to be like sedimentary rocks on Earth, which suggests that water once flowed on Mars. There could even have been oceans, long ago when the climate was milder than it is now.

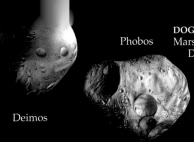

Phobos

Deimos

DOGS OF WAR
Mars has two moons, Phobos and Deimos (meaning Fear and Terror). Both are tiny—Phobos measures about 16 miles (26 km) across; Deimos, just 10 miles (16 km). Astronomers think they are asteroids that Mars captured long ago. They are dark and rich in carbon, like many asteroids.

Rockstrewn landscape of Ares Vallis region

Sojourner *Rover*

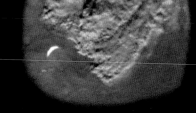

ON TOP OF THE WORLD
Olympus Mons (Mount Olympus) is the largest of four big volcanoes near Mars's equator. It rises some 15 miles (24 km) above its surroundings—nearly three times higher than Mount Everest. Measuring 370 miles (600 km) across its base, it has a summit caldera (crater) 56 miles (90 km) wide. It probably last erupted about 25 million years ago.

MARTIAN WEATHER
Although Mars has only a slight atmosphere, strong winds often blow across the surface, reaching speeds as high as 200 mph (300 km/h). They whip up fine particles from the surface to create dust storms that can sometimes shroud the whole planet.

Deadly heat ray

Martian war machine

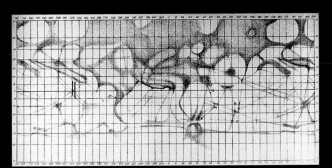

THE CANALS OF MARS
Italian astronomer Giovanni Schiaparelli first reported seeing *canali* (channels) on Mars in 1877. This led other astronomers to suppose that there was a dying Martian race digging canals to irrigate parched farmland. Prominent among them was Percival Lowell, who produced maps of the canal systems.

1907 illustration from
The War of the Worlds

THE MARTIANS ARE COMING
Thoughts of a desperate Martian race, fighting to survive in an increasingly hostile climate, stimulated the imaginations of many people, including English author H.G. Wells. In 1898, he published a groundbreaking science fiction novel entitled *The War of the Worlds*. It featured a Martian invasion of Earth, with terrifying, invincible war machines and weapons. A masterly radio adaptation of the invasion by Orson Welles, presented as though it were a news report, created a minor panic in the United States in 1938.

Jupiter, king of the planets

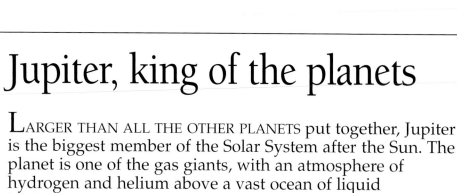

LARGER THAN ALL THE OTHER PLANETS put together, Jupiter is the biggest member of the Solar System after the Sun. The planet is one of the gas giants, with an atmosphere of hydrogen and helium above a vast ocean of liquid hydrogen. Its colorful face is crossed by dark and pale bands, called belts and zones. These are clouds that have been drawn out by the planet's rapid rotation—Jupiter spins around once in less than 10 hours. This high-speed spin also causes the planet to bulge noticeably around its equator. At least 39 moons circle the planet, but only the four so-called Galilean moons are large. Jupiter also has a ring system around it, but it is small and much too faint to be seen from Earth.

RULER OF THE GODS
Jupiter is an appropriate name for the king of the planets, because Jupiter was the king of the gods in Roman mythology. The ancient Greeks called him Zeus and told stories of his many amorous conquests. All Jupiter's moons except one (Amalthea) have been named after Zeus's lovers.

Antenna sends data back to Earth and receives instructions

Heat from nuclear fuel powers the spacecraft

Science instruments

GALILEO TO JUPITER
The US space probe *Galileo* went into orbit around Jupiter in 1995 after a five-year journey through space, using gravity boosts from Venus and Earth. *Galileo* confirmed that the top layer of Jupiter's clouds consists of ammonia ice; it detected winds in the atmosphere speeding at 400 mph (650 km/h); and it took pictures of Europa that suggest the moon may have a warm ocean beneath its surface ice.

Earth to same scale

GREAT RED SPOT
Jupiter's Great Red Spot has been seen for more than 300 years. It seems to be a super-hurricane, with winds swirling around counterclockwise at high speeds. The Spot towers 5 miles (8 km) above the surrounding cloud tops as the swirling currents rise. It changes in size, but averages about 25,000 miles (40,000 km) across. Its vivid red color is probably due to the presence of phosphorus or perhaps carbon compounds.

TARGET JUPITER
In July 1994, the 20 or so fragments of Comet Shoemaker-Levy 9 smashed into Jupiter after the giant planet had disrupted the comet's orbit. The impacts created huge fireballs in the atmosphere up to 2,500 miles (4,000 km) across. The "scars" persisted for weeks.

The plume (bottom) and the developing scar made by the impact of a comet fragment

Sulfur-covered surface

IO
The most colorful moon in the Solar System, Io is covered with flows of sulfur from many volcanoes. Volcanic eruptions send plumes of sulfur dioxide gas shooting 150 miles (250 km) above the surface. With a diameter of 2,264 miles (3,643 km), Io is about the same size as the Moon.

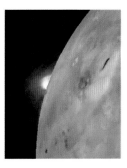

Volcanic eruption on Io

Europa's surface reflects light well

EUROPA
Europa, diameter 1,945 miles (3,130 km), has a relatively smooth, icy surface. A network of grooves and ridges crisscrosses the surface, showing where the icy crust has cracked. Astronomers think that a liquid ocean could lie beneath the ice and might contain life of some kind. Both Europa and Io are heated up by the gravitational tug of Jupiter.

Cracks in Europa's surface ice

Light areas seem to show where ice has welled up from inside Ganymede

GANYMEDE
Ganymede, diameter 3,273 miles (5,268 km), is not only Jupiter's biggest moon, but also the biggest in the whole Solar System. It is even bigger than the planet Mercury. Ganymede has an old, icy surface, with dark areas and paler grooved regions. Craters are widespread, with recent ones showing up white, where fresh ice has been exposed. Astronomers believe that Ganymede probably has a core of molten iron, like Earth.

Dark regions of older surface

CALLISTO
Callisto orbits further out than Ganymede and is a little smaller (diameter 2,986 miles / 4,806 km). It looks quite different, being almost completely covered with craters. Its crust is thought to be very ancient, dating back billions of years. From variations detected in the moon's magnetism, astronomers think that there might be a salty ocean underneath its icy crust.

Dark surface

Bright craters reveal fresh ice below surface

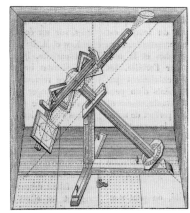

GALILEO'S MOONS
Italian astronomer Galileo Galilei was among the first to observe the heavens through a telescope (above) in 1609. He saw mountains on the Moon, sunspots, and Venus's phases. He also saw the four biggest moons of Jupiter, which are now known as the Galilean moons.

Saturn, the ringed wonder

Saturn is everyone's favorite planet because of the glorious system of shining rings that girdles its equator. Three other planets have rings—Jupiter, Uranus, and Neptune—but they are no rival to Saturn's. In the Solar System, Saturn is the sixth planet from the Sun, orbiting at an average distance of about 887 million miles (1.43 billion km). The second largest planet after Jupiter, it measures 74,900 miles (120,540 km) across at the equator. Saturn is made up mainly of hydrogen and helium around a rocky core, like Jupiter, but is even less dense. Indeed, Saturn is so light that it would float in water. In appearance, the planet's surface is a pale imitation of Jupiter's, with faint bands of clouds drawn out by its rapid rotation.

THE RING CYCLE
Saturn's axis is tilted in space at an angle of nearly 27 degrees. Because of this, we see the ring system at various angles during the planet's journey around the Sun. Twice during the near-30-year orbit, the rings lie edge-on to Earth, and almost disappear from view.

B ring

Shadow cast by Saturn across rings

F ring

Shadow of rings on planet

INSIDE THE RINGS
Pictures taken by the *Voyager* probes show that Saturn's rings are made up of thousands of narrow ringlets. The ringlets are formed from chunks of matter whizzing round in orbit at high speed. These chunks are made of ice, and vary widely in size from particles the size of sand grains to lumps as big as boulders.

RING WORLD
Through telescopes, astronomers can make out three rings around Saturn—working inward, these are the A, B, and C rings. Overall, the ring system measures about 170,000 miles (275,000 km) in diameter. The broadest and brightest ring is the B ring, while the faintest is the C ring (also called the Crepe ring). The B ring is separated from the A ring by the Cassini Division, and there is a smaller gap, called the Encke Division, near the edge of the A ring. The space probes *Pioneer 11* and *Voyagers 1* and *2* discovered several other rings—a very faint D ring extends from the C ring nearly down to Saturn's cloud tops, and F, G, and E rings lie beyond the A ring.

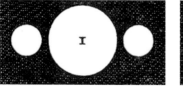

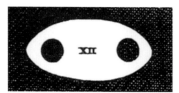

MYSTERY PLANET
Early astronomers were puzzled by Saturn's strange appearance. In his book *Systema Saturnium* (1659), Dutch astronomer Christiaan Huygens showed drawings of Saturn by astronomers from Galileo (I) onward, and examined various explanations of its unusual appearance. Huygens concluded that the planet was in fact surrounded by a thin, flat ring.

GIOVANNI CASSINI
Late 17th century astronomers believed that Saturn's rings must be solid or liquid. But doubts emerged in 1675, when Italian astronomer Giovanni Domenico Cassini (1625–1712) discovered a dark line in Saturn's rings. This proved to be a gap between two rings, and became known as the Cassini Division. Cassini realized then that the rings couldn't be solid, but their true structure was not resolved until the 19th century.

Saturn's rapid rotation makes it bulge out at the equator

STORM WORLD
The bands in Saturn's atmosphere are streams of gases coursing around the planet at high speeds and in opposite directions. At the boundary between streams, the atmosphere gets churned up and furious storms break out. This false-color picture highlights three such regions.

B ring

Cassini division

SNOW WHITE
With a diameter of about 310 miles (500 km), Enceladus is the sixth largest of Saturn's 30 or so moons and by far the brightest. Parts of its icy surface are cratered and crisscrossed with grooves, but much of it is very smooth, where the ice must recently have melted.

D ring

C ring

Inner A ring

Encke division

Outer A ring

Thick orange clouds block our view of Titan's surface

PLANET-SIZED TITAN
Saturn's largest moon, Titan, is huge. With a diameter of 3,200 miles (5,150 km), it is bigger than Mercury and second only to Ganymede among the Solar System's moons. It is also unique among moons because it is covered with a thick atmosphere that we can only see through in infrared radiation.

Infrared map of Titan's surface.

UNDER THE CLOUDS
Titan's atmosphere is mainly nitrogen, with traces of other gases, including methane (natural gas). At temperatures of –180°C (–290°F), methane rain and snow might be falling into lakes of liquid methane or onto cliffs of methane ice. The *Huygens* space probe will reveal more when it lands on Titan in 2005.

New worlds

FOR CENTURIES, NO ONE seriously thought there might be planets too faint to see with the naked eye, lying in the darkness beyond Saturn. But in March 1781, musician-turned-astronomer William Herschel discovered one. Later named Uranus, this seventh planet proved to orbit the Sun at a distance of 1.79 billion miles (2.88 billion km), twice as far away as Saturn. Suddenly, Herschel's discovery had doubled the size of the known Solar System! Oddities in Uranus's orbit suggested that another planet's gravity might be at work. This planet, Neptune, was eventually discovered by Johann Galle at Berlin Observatory in 1846. Much later, in 1930, Clyde Tombaugh of Lowell Observatory in Arizona discovered a ninth planet, tiny Pluto.

A WORLD ON EDGE
Uranus is the third largest planet, with a diameter of about 31,770 miles (51,120 km). It is a near-twin of Neptune both in size and in composition—both have deep atmospheres with warm oceans beneath. But they differ in one important respect. Neptune spins around in space more or less upright as it orbits the Sun, but Uranus has its axis tilted over, so it is nearly spinning on its side.

Almost featureless atmosphere

Methane colors the atmosphere blue-green

Uranus's tilt means its poles have a day as long as 84 Earth years

Temperature at cloud tops –345°F (–210°C)

Hydrogen and helium are the main gases in the atmosphere

DEEP-SPACE EXPLORER
Most of our detailed knowledge about the twin planets Uranus and Neptune has come from the *Voyager 2* probe. Launched in 1977, it spent 12 years visiting the four gas-giant planets. After Jupiter and Saturn, it sped past Uranus in 1986 and Neptune three years later. By the time it reached Neptune, *Voyager 2* had journeyed for 4.4 billion miles (7 billion km)—and it was still working perfectly.

Cameras

Science instruments

Dish antenna

Magnetometer boom

Miranda

Tracklike surfaces

Cracked crust

CRAZED MOONS
Uranus has at least 17 moons. Made up of rock and ice, they are all distinctly different. Ariel has deep cracks running across its surface. Miranda has all kinds of different surface features jumbled together. Some astronomers think this moon once broke apart, then came together again.

Ariel

Dark spots are lower in atmosphere than bright, high-speed "scooters"

BLUE PLANET

Neptune lies 1 billion miles (1.6 billion km) beyond Uranus. It is slightly smaller than its inner neighbor, with a diameter of 30,780 miles (49,530 km), and has a fainter ring system. The atmosphere is flecked with bright clouds and sometimes with dark oval storm regions, and is bluer than Uranus because it contains more methane. *Voyager 2* recorded a huge storm there in 1989. For Neptune to have so much atmospheric activity, it must have some kind of internal heating. This heat also keeps Neptune's cloud-tops at the same temperature as Uranus's, even though it is very much farther from the Sun.

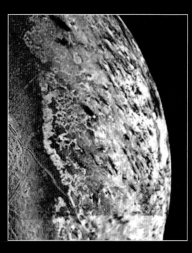

Temperature at cloud tops –345°F (–210°C)

TRITON'S GEYSERS

Triton is by far the largest of Neptune's eight moons, 1,680 miles (2,710 km) across. It is a deep-frozen world, similar to Pluto, and both are probably large members of a swarm of icy bodies that orbits beyond Neptune. Triton's surface is covered with frozen nitrogen and methane, and, amazingly, has geysers erupting on it. The geysers don't spurt out steam and water, of course, but nitrogen gas and dust.

FINDING NEPTUNE

Johann Galle first observed Neptune in 1846 after French mathematician Urbain Leverrier (1811–1877) had calculated where it should be found. John Couch Adams (1819–1892) of England had made similar calculations a year earlier, but no one had acted upon them.

Uranus has a total of 11 rings around its equator

RÉPUBLIQUE FRANÇAISE
POSTES
12F
1811 LE VERRIER 1877

Ring particles average about 3 feet (1 m) across

Charon circles around Pluto every 6 days 9 hours

ICY OUTCASTS

Pluto is smaller than Earth's Moon, measuring only 1,413 miles (2,274 km) across. Yet it has a moon of its own, Charon, which is half its size. Both bodies are made up of rock and ice, with frozen nitrogen and methane covering their surfaces. Pluto isn't always the outermost planet—for 20 years of its 248-year orbit, it comes closer to the Sun than Neptune. Pluto was last inside Neptune's orbit in 1999.

Outer ring is brightest

Pluto lies an average of 3.67 billion miles (5.9 billion km) from the Sun

Asteroids, meteors, and meteorites

THE SOLAR SYSTEM has many members besides planets and their moons. The largest are the rocky lumps we call asteroids or minor planets, orbiting relatively close to the Sun. Swarms of smaller icy bodies lurk much farther away, at the edge of the Solar System. Some occasionally travel in toward the Sun, where they melt, release clouds of gas and dust, and become visible as comets (see p.40). Asteroids often collide and chip pieces off one another, and comets leave swaths of dust in their wake. Asteroid and comet particles, called meteoroids, fill interplanetary space. When they cross Earth's orbit and enter its atmosphere, most burn up in the atmosphere as shooting stars, also termed meteors. A rare meteor that reaches the ground is called a meteorite.

Asteroid Ida

THE ASTEROID BELT
More than 10,000 asteroids have been discovered, but there are billions all together. Most of them circle the Sun in a broad band roughly midway between the orbits of Mars and Jupiter. We call this band the Asteroid Belt. The center of the belt lies roughly 250 million miles (400 million km) from the Sun. Some asteroids, however, stray outside the belt, following orbits that can take them inside Earth's orbit or out beyond Saturn's.

ASTEROID VARIETY
Even the largest asteroid, Ceres, is only about 580 miles (930 km) across, which makes it less than one-third the size of the Moon. The next largest, Pallas and Vesta, are only about half the size of Ceres. But most asteroids are very much smaller—Ida, for example, is about 35 miles (56 km) long; Gaspra only about 11 miles (18 km). These were the first asteroids photographed, by the *Galileo* spacecraft on its way to Jupiter. Gaspra is made up mostly of silicate rocks, like many asteroids. Ida's structure is more of a mystery. Other asteroids are mainly metal, or a mixture of rock and metal.

Sample of nickel-iron meteorite

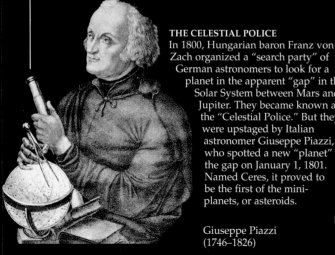

THE CELESTIAL POLICE
In 1800, Hungarian baron Franz von Zach organized a "search party" of German astronomers to look for a planet in the apparent "gap" in the Solar System between Mars and Jupiter. They became known as the "Celestial Police." But they were upstaged by Italian astronomer Giuseppe Piazzi, who spotted a new "planet" in the gap on January 1, 1801. Named Ceres, it proved to be the first of the mini-planets, or asteroids.

Giuseppe Piazzi
(1746–1826)

ASTEROID MINING
The metallic asteroids are rich in iron, as well as nickel and other metals that are comparatively rare on Earth. Metals in asteroids exist in pure form, not in ores as on Earth, and this makes them much easier to extract. So when supplies of these rarer metals start to run out, we might send astronauts or robotic mining machines into space to mine the asteroids and send their materials back to Earth. Near-Earth asteroids, the ones that come closest to our planet, would be the first targets.

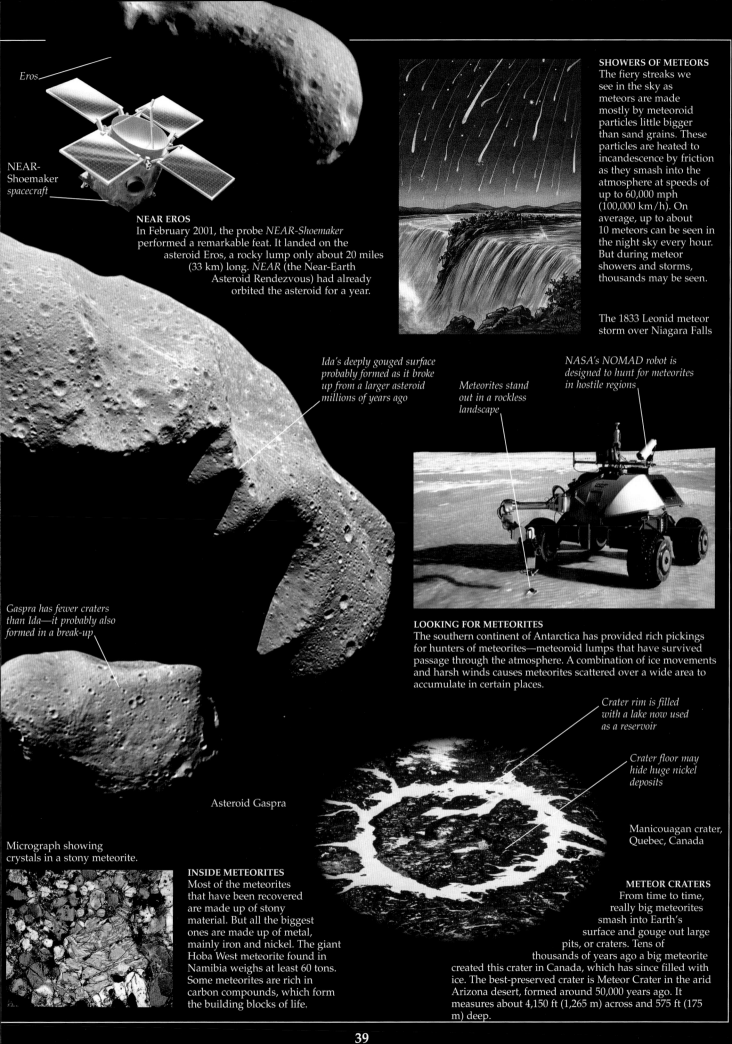

Eros

NEAR-
Shoemaker
spacecraft

NEAR EROS
In February 2001, the probe *NEAR-Shoemaker*
performed a remarkable feat. It landed on the
asteroid Eros, a rocky lump only about 20 miles
(33 km) long. *NEAR* (the Near-Earth
Asteroid Rendezvous) had already
orbited the asteroid for a year.

SHOWERS OF METEORS
The fiery streaks we
see in the sky as
meteors are made
mostly by meteoroid
particles little bigger
than sand grains. These
particles are heated to
incandescence by friction
as they smash into the
atmosphere at speeds of
up to 60,000 mph
(100,000 km/h). On
average, up to about
10 meteors can be seen in
the night sky every hour.
But during meteor
showers and storms,
thousands may be seen.

The 1833 Leonid meteor
storm over Niagara Falls

*Ida's deeply gouged surface
probably formed as it broke
up from a larger asteroid
millions of years ago*

*NASA's NOMAD robot is
designed to hunt for meteorites
in hostile regions*

*Meteorites stand
out in a rockless
landscape*

LOOKING FOR METEORITES
The southern continent of Antarctica has provided rich pickings
for hunters of meteorites—meteoroid lumps that have survived
passage through the atmosphere. A combination of ice movements
and harsh winds causes meteorites scattered over a wide area to
accumulate in certain places.

*Gaspra has fewer craters
than Ida—it probably also
formed in a break-up*

*Crater rim is filled
with a lake now used
as a reservoir*

*Crater floor may
hide huge nickel
deposits*

Asteroid Gaspra

Manicouagan crater,
Quebec, Canada

Micrograph showing
crystals in a stony meteorite.

INSIDE METEORITES
Most of the meteorites
that have been recovered
are made up of stony
material. But all the biggest
ones are made up of metal,
mainly iron and nickel. The giant
Hoba West meteorite found in
Namibia weighs at least 60 tons.
Some meteorites are rich in
carbon compounds, which form
the building blocks of life.

METEOR CRATERS
From time to time,
really big meteorites
smash into Earth's
surface and gouge out large
pits, or craters. Tens of
thousands of years ago a big meteorite
created this crater in Canada, which has since filled with
ice. The best-preserved crater is Meteor Crater in the arid
Arizona desert, formed around 50,000 years ago. It
measures about 4,150 ft (1,265 m) across and 575 ft (175
m) deep.

Icy wanderers

IN THE OUTER REACHES of the Solar System, there are great clouds of icy debris, relics of the time the Solar System was born. From time to time, some of these chunks get disturbed and travel in toward the Sun. Averaging only about 6 miles (10 km) across, they remain invisible until they are heated up by the Sun and throw off shining clouds of gas and dust. Then they can become the most spectacular of all heavenly bodies— comets. At their brightest, comets can rival the brightest planets, and can develop tails that stretch for millions of miles. Comets seem to appear suddenly out of nowhere. In the past, people believed they were signs of misfortune and brought famine, disease, death, and destruction.

HAPPY RETURNS
In his famous painting *Adoration of the Magi*, the Florentine painter Giotto (1267–1337) included a comet as the Star of Bethlehem, based on one he had seen in 1301. Giotto's comet was in fact one of the regular appearances of Halley's Comet, whose orbit brings it close to the Sun once every 76 years. The comet has been spotted on every return since 240 BC.

Gas plume bursts out of surface

HEART OF A COMET
In March 1986, the space probe *Giotto* took spectacular close-up pictures of Halley's Comet. They showed bright jets of gas spurting out of the central nucleus. Shaped a little like a potato, it measures about 10 miles (16 km) long and about half as big across. The surface is rough, covered with what look like hills and craters. It is also very dark. Analysis of the gases coming off showed them to be 80 percent water vapor. There were also traces of carbon-based organic compounds, and some astronomers think that comets might distribute these building blocks of life around the galaxy.

Gas tail streams straight away from Sun, driven by solar wind

Dark dust coats nucleus

Gas tail glows as solar wind strikes gas from comet

Nucleus is hidden in comet's glowing coma

Dark surface absorbs heat from sunlight

FRAGILE SNOWBALLS
Like snowballs, comets are not firmly held together and often break up. Early in July 1992, a comet passed very close to Jupiter and was ripped apart by the giant planet's gravity. The following spring, the fragments were spotted by comet-watchers Carolyn and Gene Shoemaker and David Levy. It soon became evident that this fragmented comet, called Shoemaker-Levy 9, was going to collide with Jupiter, which it did in July 1994.

COMET OF THE CENTURY
In spring 1997, Earth's sky was dominated by one of the brightest comets of the 20th century. It had been discovered by US astronomers Alan Hale and Thomas Bopp two years earlier. Comet Hale-Bopp outshone all but the brightest stars and hung in the night sky for weeks. It had two well-developed tails streaming away from the bright head, or coma. There was a curved, yellowish dust tail and a straighter blue gas, or ion tail. Hale-Bopp's nucleus was 20–30 miles (30–40 km) across, making it very big for a comet.

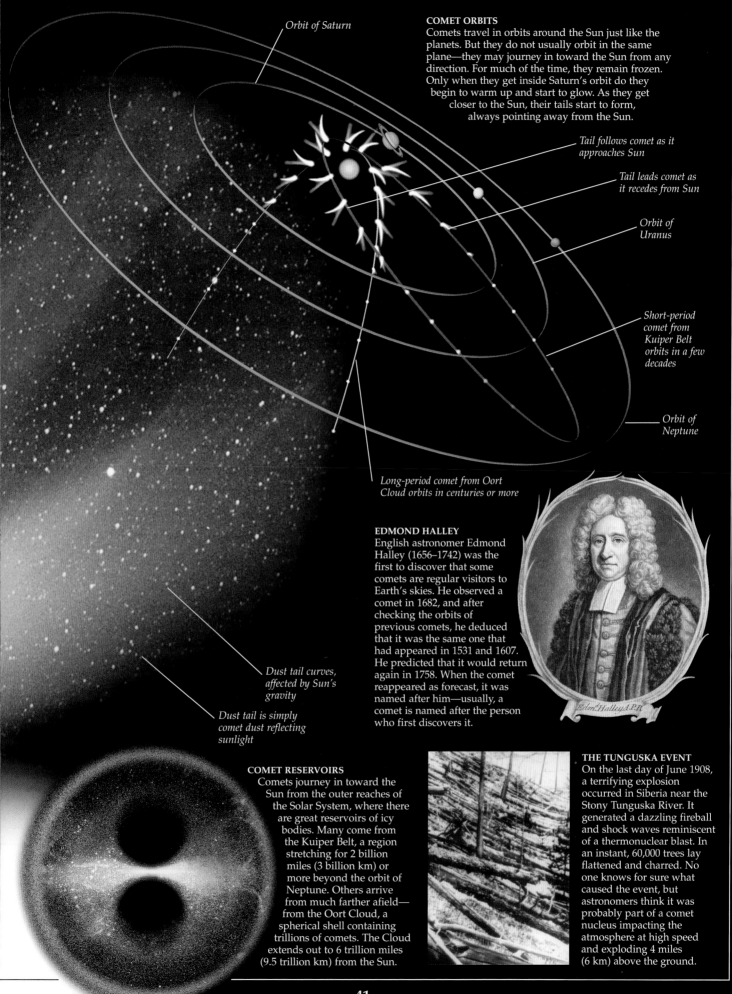

Orbit of Saturn

COMET ORBITS

Comets travel in orbits around the Sun just like the planets. But they do not usually orbit in the same plane—they may journey in toward the Sun from any direction. For much of the time, they remain frozen. Only when they get inside Saturn's orbit do they begin to warm up and start to glow. As they get closer to the Sun, their tails start to form, always pointing away from the Sun.

Tail follows comet as it approaches Sun

Tail leads comet as it recedes from Sun

Orbit of Uranus

Short-period comet from Kuiper Belt orbits in a few decades

Orbit of Neptune

Long-period comet from Oort Cloud orbits in centuries or more

EDMOND HALLEY

English astronomer Edmond Halley (1656–1742) was the first to discover that some comets are regular visitors to Earth's skies. He observed a comet in 1682, and after checking the orbits of previous comets, he deduced that it was the same one that had appeared in 1531 and 1607. He predicted that it would return again in 1758. When the comet reappeared as forecast, it was named after him—usually, a comet is named after the person who first discovers it.

Edm.ª Halley A.P.R.

Dust tail curves, affected by Sun's gravity

Dust tail is simply comet dust reflecting sunlight

COMET RESERVOIRS

Comets journey in toward the Sun from the outer reaches of the Solar System, where there are great reservoirs of icy bodies. Many come from the Kuiper Belt, a region stretching for 2 billion miles (3 billion km) or more beyond the orbit of Neptune. Others arrive from much farther afield— from the Oort Cloud, a spherical shell containing trillions of comets. The Cloud extends out to 6 trillion miles (9.5 trillion km) from the Sun.

THE TUNGUSKA EVENT

On the last day of June 1908, a terrifying explosion occurred in Siberia near the Stony Tunguska River. It generated a dazzling fireball and shock waves reminiscent of a thermonuclear blast. In an instant, 60,000 trees lay flattened and charred. No one knows for sure what caused the event, but astronomers think it was probably part of a comet nucleus impacting the atmosphere at high speed and exploding 4 miles (6 km) above the ground.

Distant suns

EVERY CLEAR NIGHT, if you were very patient, you could probably count as many as 2,500 stars in the sky. Through binoculars or a small telescope, you could see millions more. They always appear as tiny, faint pinpricks of light, but if you traveled trillions of miles to look at them close up, you would find that they are huge, bright bodies like the Sun. Even the closest star (Proxima Centauri) lies so far away that its light takes over four years to reach us—we say that it lies over four light-years away. Astronomers often use the light-year—the distance light travels in a year—as a unit to measure distances to stars. They also use a unit called the parsec, which equals about 3.3 light-years.

A UNIVERSE OF STARS
In the dense star clouds of the Milky Way, stars appear crammed together by the million. There are many different kinds of stars, with different brightness, color, size, and mass. All together, in our own great galaxy—a "star island" in space—there are as many as 200 billion stars. And there are billions more galaxies like it in the Universe.

Stars of the Sagittarius Star Cloud

Star Cloud lies 25,000 light years from Earth, toward the center of the Milky Way

Gamma Cassiopeiae (615 light-years)

Epsilon Cassiopeiae (440 light-years)

Alpha Cassiopeiae (240 light-years)

Beta Cassiopeiae (54 light-years)

True distances to Cassiopeia's stars (not to scale)

Star pattern in the constellation Cassiopeia

Delta Cassiopeiae (100 light-years)

STARS AND CONSTELLATIONS
Some of the bright stars form patterns in the sky that we can recognize. We call them the constellations. Ancient astronomers named them after figures that featured in their myths and legends. The stars in the constellations look as if they are grouped together in the sky, but they usually are not. They appear together only because they happen to lie in the same direction in space. This also means that stars that seem to have the same brightness may in fact be very different.

HOW FAR AWAY?
The distance to a few hundred of the nearest stars can be measured directly by the parallax method. Parallax is the effect that makes a nearby object appear to move against a more distant background when you look at it first with one eye, then the other. Astronomers view a nearby star first from one side of Earth's orbit, then from the other. They measure the amount a star appears to move against the background of more distant stars. From these parallax shifts they can work out the star's distance.

Distant stars

Closer star B has larger parallax shift than more distant star A

Parallax shift against distant background stars

Line of sight to star B

Line of sight to star A

Earth's position in January

Earth's position in July

Sun

Betelgeuse (magnitude 0.8)

Rigel and Betelgeuse appear roughly the same brightness, but Rigel is really twice as far away and five times more luminous than Betelgeuse.

Rigel (magnitude 0.1)

STAR BRIGHTNESS
The stars in the constellations differ widely in brightness, as here in Orion. We measure brightness on a scale of magnitude introduced by the Greek astronomer Hipparchus over 2,000 years ago. He graded the brightest stars we can see as first-magnitude stars, and the dimmest ones as sixth-magnitude. Today, we extend the scale to negative magnitudes for very bright stars, and beyond 6 for stars too faint for the eye to detect.

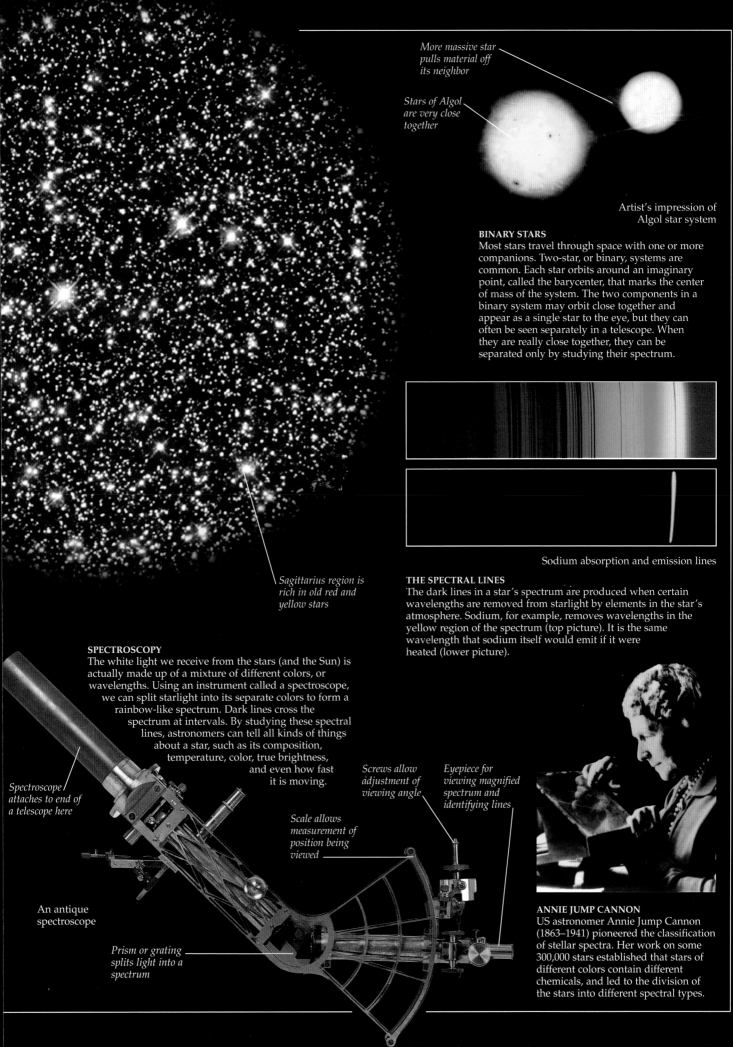

More massive star
pulls material off
its neighbor

Stars of Algol
are very close
together

Artist's impression of
Algol star system

BINARY STARS

Most stars travel through space with one or more
companions. Two-star, or binary, systems are
common. Each star orbits around an imaginary
point, called the barycenter, that marks the center
of mass of the system. The two components in a
binary system may orbit close together and
appear as a single star to the eye, but they can
often be seen separately in a telescope. When
they are really close together, they can be
separated only by studying their spectrum.

Sodium absorption and emission lines

THE SPECTRAL LINES

The dark lines in a star's spectrum are produced when certain
wavelengths are removed from starlight by elements in the star's
atmosphere. Sodium, for example, removes wavelengths in the
yellow region of the spectrum (top picture). It is the same
wavelength that sodium itself would emit if it were
heated (lower picture).

Sagittarius region is
rich in old red and
yellow stars

SPECTROSCOPY

The white light we receive from the stars (and the Sun) is
actually made up of a mixture of different colors, or
wavelengths. Using an instrument called a spectroscope,
we can split starlight into its separate colors to form a
rainbow-like spectrum. Dark lines cross the
spectrum at intervals. By studying these spectral
lines, astronomers can tell all kinds of things
about a star, such as its composition,
temperature, color, true brightness,
and even how fast
it is moving.

Screws allow
adjustment of
viewing angle

Eyepiece for
viewing magnified
spectrum and
identifying lines

Spectroscope
attaches to end of
a telescope here

Scale allows
measurement of
position being
viewed

An antique
spectroscope

ANNIE JUMP CANNON

US astronomer Annie Jump Cannon
(1863–1941) pioneered the classification
of stellar spectra. Her work on some
300,000 stars established that stars of
different colors contain different
chemicals, and led to the division of
the stars into different spectral types.

Prism or grating
splits light into a
spectrum

The variety of stars

STUDYING THE SPECTRA of stars tells us all kinds of things about them—their composition, color, temperature, speed of travel, and size. Other techniques allow astronomers to measure the distance to stars and their mass. Stars turn out to vary enormously. There are dwarfs with only a hundredth the diameter of the Sun and supergiants hundreds of times the Sun's size. The lightest stars have around one-tenth of the Sun's mass, the heaviest around 50 solar masses. The dimmest are a million times fainter than the Sun, while the brightest are a million times brighter. But there do seem to be some rules—red stars are either very faint or very bright, while most other stars tend to be brighter if they are bluer.

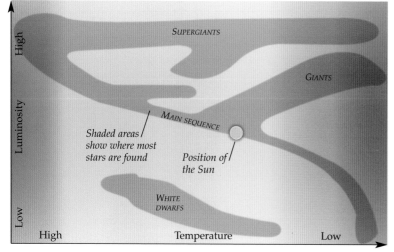

SUPERGIANTS
The biggest stars of all, hundreds of millions of miles across, relatively cool but amazingly bright

STARS LARGE AND SMALL
A range of typical stars is shown across this page. The brightest are at the top, the hottest on the left, and the coolest on the right. The true size differences are far greater than those shown, but some patterns are obvious—stars get bigger as they get brighter, and the brightest stars are either bright blue or orange-red. A star's color is governed by its surface temperature—the amount of energy pumping out of each square meter of its surface. This means that if two stars have the same brightness but one is cool and red while the other is hot and blue, then the red one must be far bigger than the blue one.

BLUE STARS
Tens of times bigger than the Sun, and tens of thousands of times brighter, with a surface temperature up to 90,000°F (50,000°C)

WHITE DWARFS
Tiny hot stars only about the size of the Earth

Line of main sequence

THE HERTZSPRUNG-RUSSELL DIAGRAM AND STELLAR EVOLUTION
The Hertzsprung-Russell (HR) diagram is a way of looking at relationships between the true brightness (luminosity) of stars and their color and temperature. The majority of stars lie along a diagonal strip from faint red to bright blue called the main sequence—this must be where most stars spend most of their lives. Stars spend much of their life close to one point on the main sequence—they only move off it toward the end of their lives, as they grow bigger and brighter.

Diagram labels:
High · Luminosity · Low
SUPERGIANTS
GIANTS
MAIN SEQUENCE
Shaded areas show where most stars are found
Position of the Sun
WHITE DWARFS
High · Temperature · Low

FIRST DWARF
Stars similar to the Sun end their lives as white dwarfs, which gradually fade away. The faint companion of Sirius, called Sirius B (left), was the first white dwarf discovered, by US astronomer Alvan Clark in 1862. It proved to be exceptionally hot and very dense.

The brightest supergiants are a million times brighter than the Sun

Star at its hottest causes outward expansion

Star at its coolest collapses back under gravity

Star oscillates back and forth through balance point

Star is brightest when at its hottest

Size and color change is exaggerated

PULSATING VARIABLES

Not all stars shine steadily. Some change in brightness—we call them variables. Pulsating variables alter their brightness as they pulsate, getting periodically bigger then smaller. They are brightest when they are small and hot, dimmest when they are large and cool. These variables are stars near the end of their lives, like the red giant star Mira.

Bright star eclipsed

Dim star eclipsed

Combined star at its brightest

Brightness drops dramatically

Brightness drops slightly

ECLIPSING VARIABLES

Eclipsing variables appear to vary in brightness for another reason. They are binary star systems in which a small bright star and a large dim star orbit around each other. They orbit in our line of sight so that each passes in front of, or eclipses, the other in turn. When this happens, the overall brightness of the system dips.

Perseus used his shield to look at Medusa when he confronted her

Medusa's gaze could turn people to stone

THE WINKING DEMON

In the constellation Perseus, a variable star named Algol marks the eye of Medusa, the snake-haired Gorgon that the Greek hero slew. Algol, often called the winking demon, dips noticeably in brightness every 2.9 days. English astronomer John Goodricke first recognized that it was an eclipsing binary in 1783.

RED GIANTS
Bright stars, but cool because of their size, typically about 30 times the size of the Sun

SUNLIKE STARS
Roughly 900,000 miles (1,500,000 km) across, with a surface temperature of around 11,000°F (6,000°C)

RED DWARFS
About 1/10th the size of the Sun, with a surface temperature of about 5,500°F (3,000°C)

The faintest red dwarfs are a million times fainter than our Sun

SUNLIKE STARS

The Sun is an average star of a type known as a yellow dwarf. Its color reflects its surface temperature, which is around 9,900°F (5,500°C). Astronomers think that the Sun is about halfway through its life, which means that it should stay on the main sequence, shining steadily, for another 5 billion years.

EJNAR HERTZSPRUNG

Ejnar Hertzsprung (1873–1967) was born in Frederiksberg, Denmark. He studied to be a chemical engineer but became an astronomer instead. He first noticed the relationship between star brightness and temperature in 1906. Working in the US, Henry Norris Russell (1877–1957) independently came to similar conclusions. Both are commemorated in the HR diagram, which is of vital importance in astronomy.

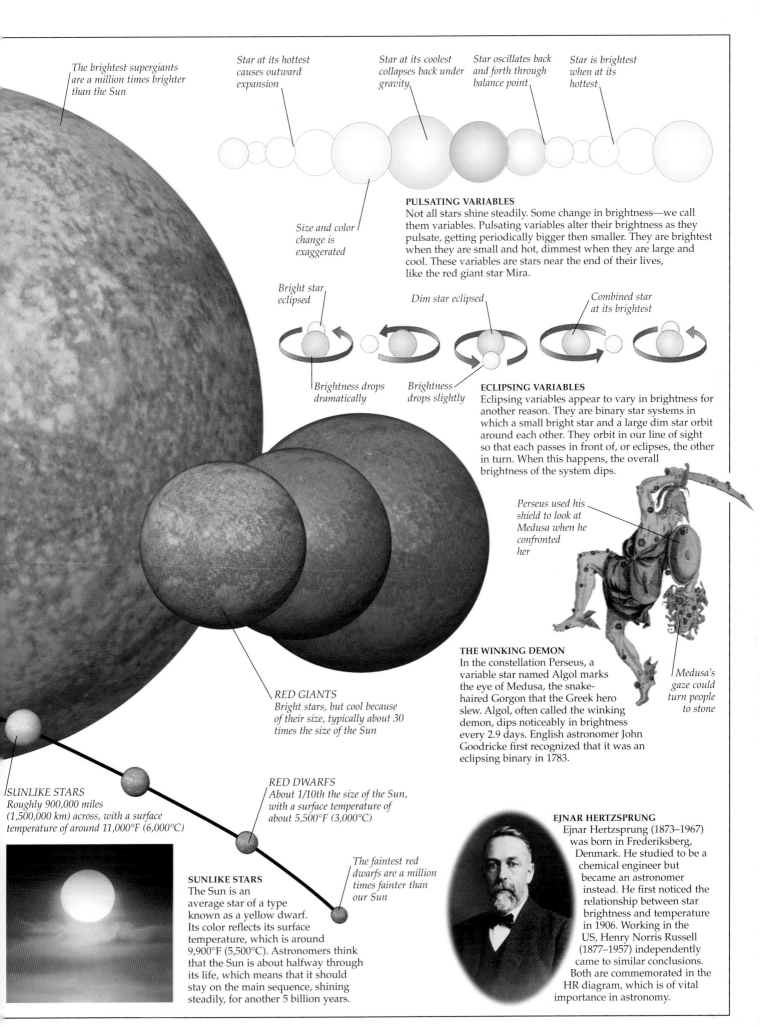

Clusters and nebulae

IN MANY PARTS OF THE HEAVENS there are fuzzy patches that look as if they might be comets. Through a telescope, some turn out to be close groupings of stars, known as clusters—in general, stars are born in groups rather than alone. Open clusters are relatively loose collections of a few hundred stars. Globular clusters are dense groupings of many thousands of stars. Other fuzzy patches turn out to be cloudlike regions of glowing gas. We call these nebulae, from the Latin word for clouds. They are the visible part of the interstellar medium, the stuff that occupies the space between the stars. The darker, denser parts of nebulae are where stars are born.

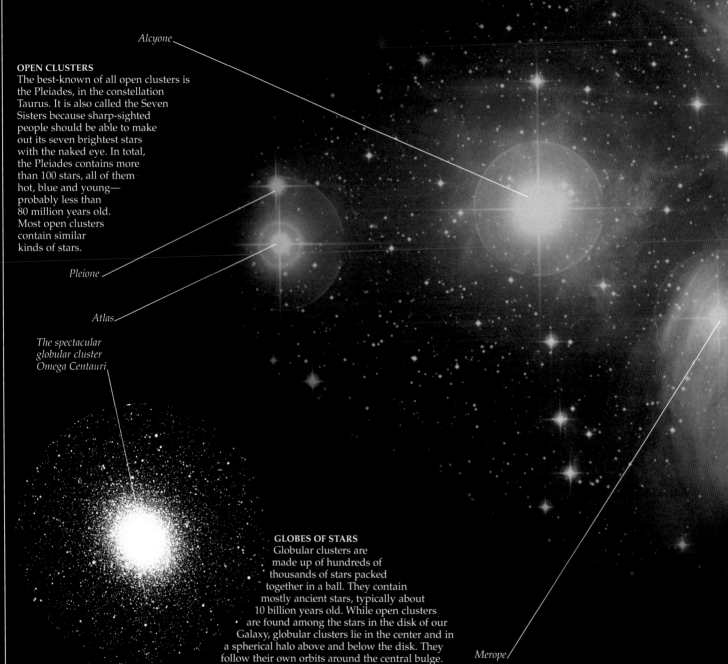

Alcyone

OPEN CLUSTERS
The best-known of all open clusters is the Pleiades, in the constellation Taurus. It is also called the Seven Sisters because sharp-sighted people should be able to make out its seven brightest stars with the naked eye. In total, the Pleiades contains more than 100 stars, all of them hot, blue and young— probably less than 80 million years old. Most open clusters contain similar kinds of stars.

Pleione

Atlas

The spectacular globular cluster Omega Centauri

GLOBES OF STARS
Globular clusters are made up of hundreds of thousands of stars packed together in a ball. They contain mostly ancient stars, typically about 10 billion years old. While open clusters are found among the stars in the disk of our Galaxy, globular clusters lie in the center and in a spherical halo above and below the disk. They follow their own orbits around the central bulge.

Merope

Between the stars

The interstellar medium is made up mainly of hydrogen gas and specks of dust. It also contains traces of many other compounds, including water, alcohol, hydrogen sulfide, and ammonia. All together, the interstellar medium accounts for a tenth of the mass of our Galaxy. It can become visible as both bright and dark nebulae.

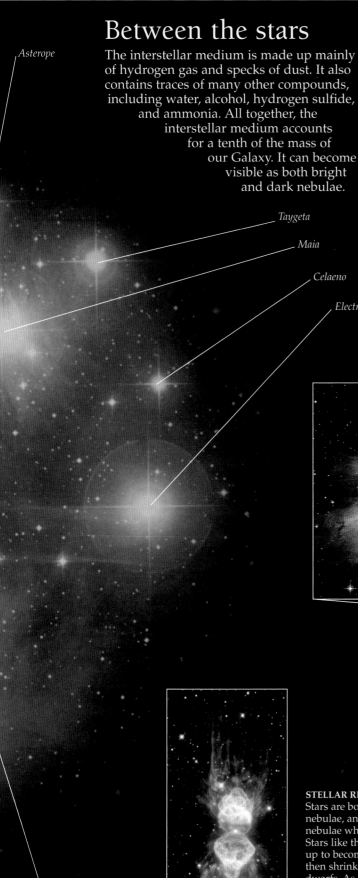

Asterope

Taygeta

Maia

Celaeno

Electra

Reflection nebula surrounding young stars

DARK NEBULAE

Some clouds of gas and dust are lit up, while others remain dark. We see dark nebulae only when they blot out the light from stars or glowing gas in the background. The aptly named Horsehead Nebula (above) is a well-known dark nebula in Orion. Another, in far southern skies, is the Coal Sack in Crux, the Southern Cross. Dark nebulae are generally cold, around –435°F (–260°C), and made up mainly of hydrogen molecules. Such molecular clouds give birth to stars.

The Orion Nebula, M42

M42's position in Orion

BRIGHT NEBULAE

Many interstellar gas clouds are lit up by stars, creating some of the most beautiful sights in the heavens. Sometimes the clouds just reflect the light from nearby stars, and we see them as reflection nebulae. Sometimes radiation from stars embedded within the clouds gives extra energy to the gas molecules, causing them to emit radiation. Then we see the clouds as emission nebulae. The famous Orion Nebula (above) is primarily an emission nebula.

STELLAR REMNANTS

Stars are born from nebulae, and give rise to nebulae when they die. Stars like the Sun first swell up to become red giants, then shrink into tiny white dwarfs. As they do so, they puff off layers of gas, which become planetary nebulae. Some of these nebulae are circular and look rather like the disks of planets; others, like the Ant Nebula, consist of luminous jets.

MESSIER'S CATALOG

French astronomer Charles Messier (1730–1817) was nicknamed the "ferret of comets" for his skill in searching for new comets. He discovered 15 in all. He also compiled a catalog in which he listed 104 star clusters and nebulae that might be mistaken for comets. The objects in the catalogue are still often identified by their Messier (M) numbers.

Star birth

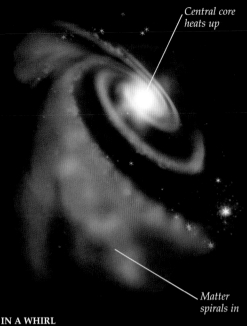

Central core
heats up

Matter
spirals in

IN A WHIRL
The molecular clouds that spawn stars move
around slowly in space. When cores of matter
collapse during star formation, they start to
rotate—the smaller they become, the faster
they spin. The collapsing matter, with the
glowing protostar inside, forms into a
disk as a result of the rotation.

Sᴛᴀʀs ᴀʀᴇ ʙᴏʀɴ in the vast, dark swathes of gas and dust
that occupy interstellar space. Called giant molecular
clouds, they are very cold (around −440°F/−260°C) and
consist mainly of hydrogen gas. In places within these
clouds, gravity pulls the gas molecules together to make
denser clumps. Within these clumps there are even denser
regions, called cores, and it is from cores that individual
stars are born. Gravity makes a core collapse in on itself,
greatly compressing the material at the center. As the
collapse continues, the central region becomes more and
more compressed and gets hotter and hotter. Now called a
protostar, it begins to glow. When its temperature reaches
around 18 million°F (10 million°C), its nuclear furnace fires
up, and it begins to shine brightly as a new star.

STELLAR NURSERIES
Stars are being born in vast numbers in giant molecular
clouds all around the heavens. M16, the Eagle Nebula
in Serpens, is one of these stellar nurseries. The
Hubble Space Telescope has taken dramatic pictures
of dark columns nicknamed "the pillars of
creation," where star formation is taking place.
This picture of the top of one pillar shows
fingerlike blobs of gas called EGGs, or
evaporating gaseous globules.

Collapsing gas
clouds

EGG

Stars are hidden
within gas

Disk more stable at greater distances from star

BIRTH PANGS
A newborn star is surrounded by a swirling disk of matter with perhaps three times its mass, but not for long. Powerful stellar winds gather up the matter and force it away from the star's poles as twin jets. This is called bipolar outflow.

JET EFFECTS
The two jets that emerge from the poles of newborn stars travel very fast—at speeds of hundreds of miles per second. As they punch their way through interstellar gas, they make it glow, creating what are called Herbig-Haro Objects. The picture shows one close to the young star Gamma Cassiopeiae.

Close to star, matter is pulled in by gravity

Disk heats up close to star

Nearby gas reflecting starlight

Stellar winds blow material out in jets

Sulfur ions glow blue when jet hits them

Central star

Hydrogen atoms glow green when struck by jet

Worlds beyond

Newborn stars blow most of the matter surrounding them into space, but usually a disk of material remains. It is from such disks that planetary systems form. Astronomers first began discovering planets around ordinary stars in 1995. Today, we know of more than 100 of these extrasolar planets, or exoplanets.

Star blacked out

Disk seen edge-on to Earth

THE HIDDEN MILLIONS
The Orion Nebula is one of the closest star-forming regions. In visible light (above left), glowing gas in the nebula hides most of the young stars. But viewed in the infrared (above right), a wealth of stars becomes visible, many of them red and brown dwarfs. Red dwarfs are small, cool stars. Brown dwarfs are the stars that never made it. They have a low mass and couldn't reach a high enough temperature for nuclear fusion to begin.

Disk of gas and dust

Star moves toward us

Barycenter

Star

Planet

Star moves away

PLANETS IN FORMATION
Space probes like *IRAS* (Infrared Astronomy Satellite) began detecting disks of material around other stars in the 1980s. One is Beta Pictoris, which is pictured above. Another is the bright star Vega in Lyra. Planets could form in these systems within a few million years.

LOOKING FOR PLANETS
The planets around other stars are much too faint to be seen directly. Astronomers have to find them indirectly, by observing the effect they have on their star. Planet and star both orbit around a shared center of gravity or barycenter, usually deep within the star but not quite at the center. During an orbit, the star appears from Earth to move repeatedly toward and away from us. We can detect this motion by examining the shift in the lines in the star's spectrum (see p.42).

GIANTS LIKE JUPITER
Astronomers detected the first extrasolar planets in 1991, orbiting a dead star called a pulsar. Four years later, a planet was found around the Sunlike 51 Pegasi. It has half the mass of Jupiter and orbits only about 6 million miles (10 million km) from its star. Most exoplanets detected so far are heavier than Jupiter, and orbit close to their stars.

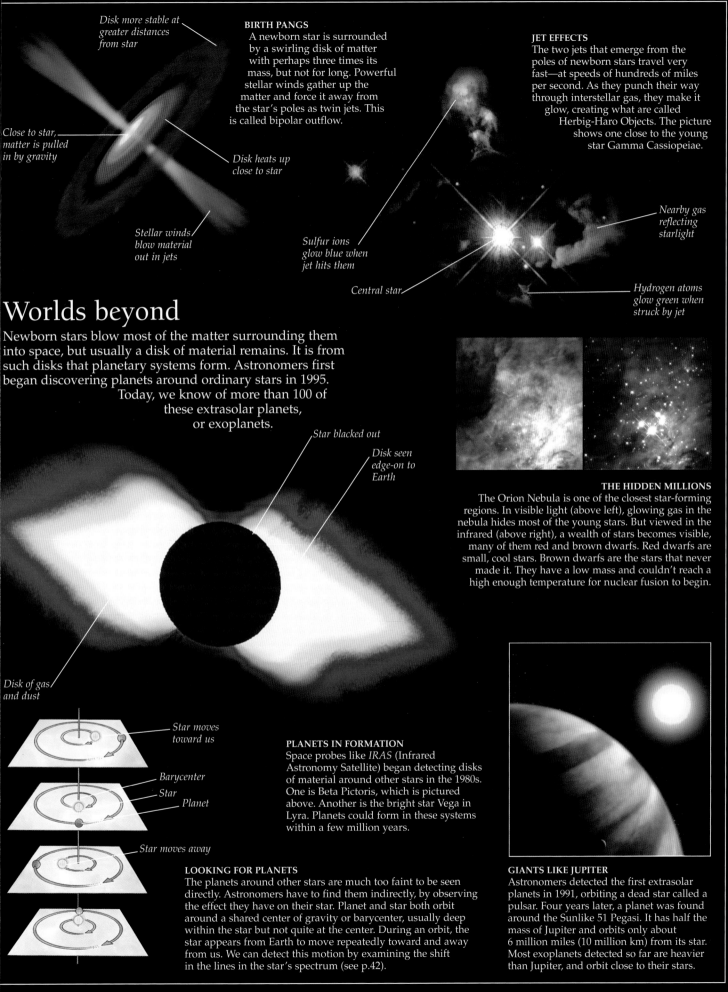

Star death

STARS BURST INTO LIFE when they begin fusing hydrogen into helium in nuclear reactions in their cores. They spend most of their lives shining steadily until they use up their hydrogen fuel—then they start to die. First they pass through a phase when they brighten and swell to enormous size as red giants and supergiants. The way a star ultimately dies depends on its mass. Low-mass stars puff off their outer layers and then fade away. High-mass stars die in a spectacular explosion called a supernova.

FATES OF STARS

A star that is burning hydrogen in its core changes its color and brightness very little. How long the star can keep burning hydrogen depends on its mass. Stars like the Sun burn their fuel slowly and so can shine steadily for up to 10 billion years.

RED GIANT

When a star has used up the hydrogen in its core, fusion moves out to a thin shell around the center. This produces so much heat that the star's atmosphere balloons outward. As it expands, its surface cools and its light reddens—it has become a red giant. Meanwhile, the inner core of helium collapses, until it is hot and dense enough for new nuclear reactions to begin. These turn helium into heavier elements, and give the star a new lease on life—for about 2 billion years.

SUPERGIANT

In stars with more than eight times the Sun's mass, the core gets so hot that carbon and oxygen, produced by helium fusion, can themselves fuse into heavier elements. The star balloons out to become a supergiant, many times larger than a normal red giant.

PLANETARY NEBULA

When all the helium in the core of a solar-mass red giant runs out, the core collapses again, releasing energy that blows the outer layers of the star into space. Radiation from the hot core makes the ejected gas light up, forming a ring-shaped planetary nebula.

LIVE FAST, DIE YOUNG

Stars more massive than the Sun have hotter, denser cores. This allows them to burn their hydrogen fuel in a much more efficient way, but also shortens their lifespans dramatically—the heaviest are stable for just a few million years.

New fusion reactions produce sodium, magnesium, silicon, sulfur, and other elements

Heaviest element produced is iron

Core not shown to scale

Core develops "onion layers"

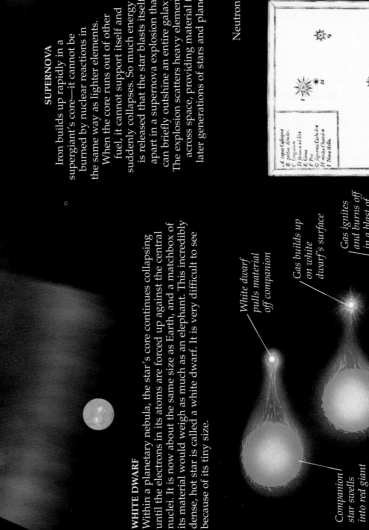

Black hole

Neutron star

SUPERNOVA

Iron builds up rapidly in a supergiant's core—it cannot be burned by nuclear reactions in the same way as lighter elements.

When the core runs out of other fuel, it cannot support itself and suddenly collapses. So much energy is released that the star blasts itself apart in a supernova explosion that can briefly outshine an entire galaxy. The explosion scatters heavy elements across space, providing material for later generations of stars and planets.

END STATES

What survives after a supernova depends on the mass of the collapsing core. If the core has less than about three solar masses, it will shrink to an incredibly dense neutron star. If the core has a greater mass, it will end up as a black hole and vanish forever from the visible Universe (see p.52).

SUPERNOVA 1987A

On February 23, 1987, astronomers spotted a bright supernova in the Large Magellanic Cloud, one of the closest galaxies to our own. It flared up over 85 days to become easily visible to the naked eye. The star that exploded was a blue giant called Sanduleak −69°202, with about 20 times the mass of the Sun.

SUPERNOVAE IN HISTORY

Tycho Brahe saw a supernova in 1572 (shown above), which caused him to realize that the heavens were not unchanging. But the most famous historical supernova is probably the one Chinese astronomers saw in 1054; today its remains form the Crab Nebula in the constellation Taurus.

WHITE DWARF

Within a planetary nebula, the star's core continues collapsing until the electrons in its atoms are forced up against the central nuclei. It is now about the same size as Earth, and a matchbox of its material would weigh as much as an elephant. This incredibly dense, hot star is called a white dwarf. It is very difficult to see because of its tiny size.

Companion star swells into red giant

White dwarf pulls material off companion

Gas builds up on white dwarf's surface

Gas ignites and burns off in a blast of fusion

Companion is caught in blast

NOVAE

When a white dwarf forms in a close binary star system, it may attract gas from the other star. Over time, gas builds up on the white dwarf's surface until it is hot and dense enough to trigger nuclear fusion. A gigantic explosion takes place that makes the star flare up and become a nova, an apparently new star.

Pulsars and black holes

WHEN A MASSIVE STAR DIES in a supernova (see p.50), only the core is left behind, collapsed under its own enormous gravity. The force as the core collapses is so great that atoms are broken down. Negatively charged electrons are forced into the central nucleus of each atom, combining with positively charged protons to turn all the matter into tightly packed neutrons that have no electric charge. The collapsed core becomes a city-sized neutron star, spinning furiously as it emits pulses of radiation. When we detect the pulses from a neutron star, we call it a pulsar. Collapsing cores with more than three solar masses suffer a different fate. The force of collapse is so great that even neutrons get crushed. Eventually, the core is so dense that not even light can escape its gravity—it has become that most mysterious of bodies, a black hole.

THE CRAB PULSAR
In the year 1054, Chinese astronomers recorded seeing a star in the constellation Taurus bright enough to be visible in daylight. We now know that it was a supernova explosion, which created the famous Crab Nebula. Buried inside the nebula is the collapsed core, which we detect as a pulsar.

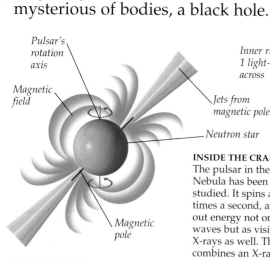

Pulsar's rotation axis

Magnetic field

Inner ring 1 light-year across

Jets from magnetic poles

Neutron star

Magnetic pole

INSIDE THE CRAB
The pulsar in the Crab Nebula has been closely studied. It spins around 30 times a second, and pours out energy not only as radio waves but as visible light and X-rays as well. This picture combines an X-ray image from the Chandra X-Ray Observatory satellite (in blue) with a visible light photo.

Jet from pulsar poles

Pulsar jet billows into clouds as it contacts interstellar gas

Material blown out from equator reaches half the speed of light

Neutron star

NEUTRON STARS
Neutron stars are tiny bodies that spin around rapidly. The fastest one known spins 642 times a second. They are highly magnetic, so their magnetic field sweeps around rapidly as well. This generates radio waves, which are emitted as beams from the magnetic poles. When the beams sweep past Earth, we see them as pulsing signals, rather like the flashes from a lighthouse.

SUPERDENSE MATTER
A neutron star is typically only around 12 miles (20 km) across. Yet it contains the mass of up to three Suns. This makes it incredibly dense. Just a pinhead of neutron-star matter would weigh twice as much as the world's heaviest supertanker. It is unlike any kind of matter found on Earth.

PULSAR DISCOVERY
Working at Cambridge University, England, in 1967, research student Jocelyn Bell Burnell (born 1943) was testing new equipment to study fluctuating radio sources. On August 6, she picked up signals pulsating every 1.337 seconds. It was the first pulsar to be found, now called PSR 1919+21.

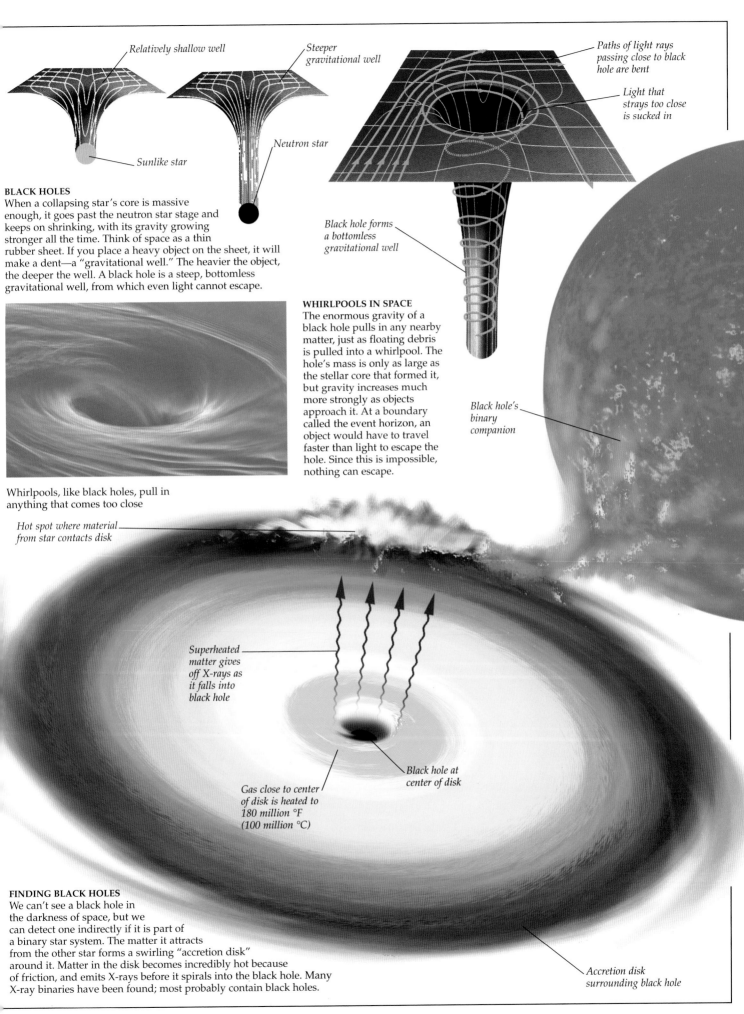

Relatively shallow well

Steeper gravitational well

Sunlike star

Neutron star

Paths of light rays passing close to black hole are bent

Light that strays too close is sucked in

BLACK HOLES

When a collapsing star's core is massive enough, it goes past the neutron star stage and keeps on shrinking, with its gravity growing stronger all the time. Think of space as a thin rubber sheet. If you place a heavy object on the sheet, it will make a dent—a "gravitational well." The heavier the object, the deeper the well. A black hole is a steep, bottomless gravitational well, from which even light cannot escape.

Black hole forms a bottomless gravitational well

WHIRLPOOLS IN SPACE

The enormous gravity of a black hole pulls in any nearby matter, just as floating debris is pulled into a whirlpool. The hole's mass is only as large as the stellar core that formed it, but gravity increases much more strongly as objects approach it. At a boundary called the event horizon, an object would have to travel faster than light to escape the hole. Since this is impossible, nothing can escape.

Black hole's binary companion

Whirlpools, like black holes, pull in anything that comes too close

Hot spot where material from star contacts disk

Superheated matter gives off X-rays as it falls into black hole

Gas close to center of disk is heated to 180 million °F (100 million °C)

Black hole at center of disk

Accretion disk surrounding black hole

FINDING BLACK HOLES

We can't see a black hole in the darkness of space, but we can detect one indirectly if it is part of a binary star system. The matter it attracts from the other star forms a swirling "accretion disk" around it. Matter in the disk becomes incredibly hot because of friction, and emits X-rays before it spirals into the black hole. Many X-ray binaries have been found; most probably contain black holes.

The Milky Way

ON A CLEAR, DARK NIGHT, a faint, hazy band of light arches across the heavens, running through many of the best-known constellations. We call it the Milky Way. What we are seeing is a kind of "slice" through the star system, or galaxy, to which the Sun and all the other stars in the sky belong. It passes through Cygnus, Perseus, and Cassiopeia in the northern hemisphere, and Centaurus, Crux, and Sagittarius in the southern hemisphere. When you look at the Milky Way through binoculars or a telescope, you can see that it is made up of countless stars, seemingly packed close together. We also call our star system the Milky Way Galaxy, or just the Galaxy. It has a spiral shape, with star-studded "arms" curving out from a dense bulge of stars in the middle.

MILKY WAY MYTHS
In the mythology of the Aztecs of Mexico, the Milky Way was identified with Mixcoatl, the cloud-serpent god. In ancient Egypt and India, it was seen as the celestial mirror of rivers like the Nile and Ganges. The Greeks believed it was a stream of milk from the breast of the goddess Hera, wife of Zeus the ruler of the gods

ANATOMY OF THE GALAXY
Our Galaxy is a vast system of around 200 billion stars. It measures 100,000 light-years across, but for the most part is only about 2,000 light-years thick. The spiral arms around the central bulge form the disk of the Galaxy. There are two major arms, the Sagittarius and the Perseus, named for the constellations where they appear brightest. Between the two lies the Orion, or Local Arm, on which the Sun lies, 26,000 light years from the galactic center.

Star-forming molecular clouds

Milky Way star clouds in Scorpius and Sagittarius

Orion arm

THE BACKBONE OF NIGHT
The Milky Way is best seen on clear, moonless nights away from urban light pollution. Its brightest areas are most visible between June and September. The dark patches, or rifts, in the Milky Way are not starless regions, but areas in which dense dust clouds block the light from the stars behind them.

Location of our Solar System

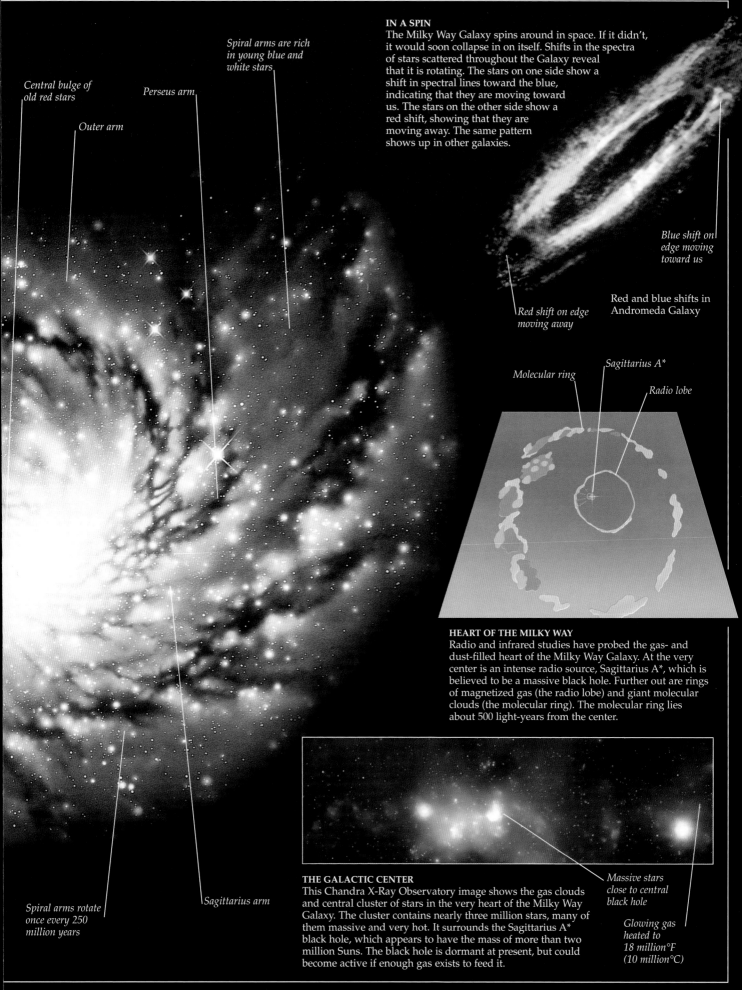

Central bulge of old red stars

Perseus arm

Outer arm

Spiral arms are rich in young blue and white stars

IN A SPIN

The Milky Way Galaxy spins around in space. If it didn't, it would soon collapse in on itself. Shifts in the spectra of stars scattered throughout the Galaxy reveal that it is rotating. The stars on one side show a shift in spectral lines toward the blue, indicating that they are moving toward us. The stars on the other side show a red shift, showing that they are moving away. The same pattern shows up in other galaxies.

Blue shift on edge moving toward us

Red shift on edge moving away

Red and blue shifts in Andromeda Galaxy

Molecular ring

Sagittarius A*

Radio lobe

HEART OF THE MILKY WAY

Radio and infrared studies have probed the gas- and dust-filled heart of the Milky Way Galaxy. At the very center is an intense radio source, Sagittarius A*, which is believed to be a massive black hole. Further out are rings of magnetized gas (the radio lobe) and giant molecular clouds (the molecular ring). The molecular ring lies about 500 light-years from the center.

THE GALACTIC CENTER

This Chandra X-Ray Observatory image shows the gas clouds and central cluster of stars in the very heart of the Milky Way Galaxy. The cluster contains nearly three million stars, many of them massive and very hot. It surrounds the Sagittarius A* black hole, which appears to have the mass of more than two million Suns. The black hole is dormant at present, but could become active if enough gas exists to feed it.

Massive stars close to central black hole

Glowing gas heated to 18 million°F (10 million°C)

Sagittarius arm

Spiral arms rotate once every 250 million years

Neighbors

IN FAR SOUTHERN SKIES, two misty patches can be seen in the constellations Tucana and Dorado. They are called the Large and Small Magellanic Clouds. They are not, as was once thought, clouds or nebulae in our own Galaxy—instead, they are separate star systems, neighboring galaxies. The Large Magellanic Cloud lies just 160,000 light-years away, a mere stone's throw in space. It is small compared with our Galaxy and is irregular in shape, as is the Small Magellanic Cloud. The Magellanic Clouds and a number of smaller dwarf elliptical galaxies are not just neighbors of the Milky Way; they also come under its gravitational influence. In turn, the Milky Way and its satellites are bound by gravity into the Local Group, a family of galaxies some 3 million light-years across.

MAGELLAN'S CLOUDS
The Magellanic Clouds are named after Portuguese navigator Ferdinand Magellan (1480–1521). He commanded the first expedition to voyage around the world, which set out in 1519. He was one of the first Europeans to see the clouds, and probably used them to navigate.

Small Magellanic Cloud

Large Magellanic Cloud

THE LOCAL GROUP
The Milky Way and its satellite galaxies form part of a much larger collection of galaxies called the Local Group. This group also includes two more spiral galaxies in the constellations Andromeda and Triangulum. All the other galaxies are elliptical or irregular galaxies, and are very much smaller. In all, there are about 30 galaxies in the Local Group, bound loosely together by gravity. In turn, the group forms part of a much larger cluster of galaxies.

SATELLITE GALAXIES
The Large Magellanic Cloud is 30,000 light-years across, less than one-third the size of the Milky Way. It contains much the same mix of stars and gas as our own Galaxy, but has no features like a central bulge or spiral arms. It does have a broad band of relatively old stars, and also vast star-forming regions, such as the Tarantula Nebula. This nebula is one of the biggest and brightest known, lit up by a cluster of young, hot, massive stars. The Small Magellanic Cloud is only a quarter as massive as the Large Cloud and lies slightly farther away, 190,000 light-years from Earth.

OUR CANNIBAL GALAXY
There is a tiny galaxy even closer to us than the Large Magellanic Cloud. The Sagittarius Dwarf Elliptical lies 80,000 light-years away, hidden behind the dense gas clouds in the center of our Galaxy and only discovered in 1994. Originally spherical, the galaxy is being pulled apart by the Milky Way's gravity. Over time, it will be swallowed up by our Galaxy, as will the Magellanic Clouds.

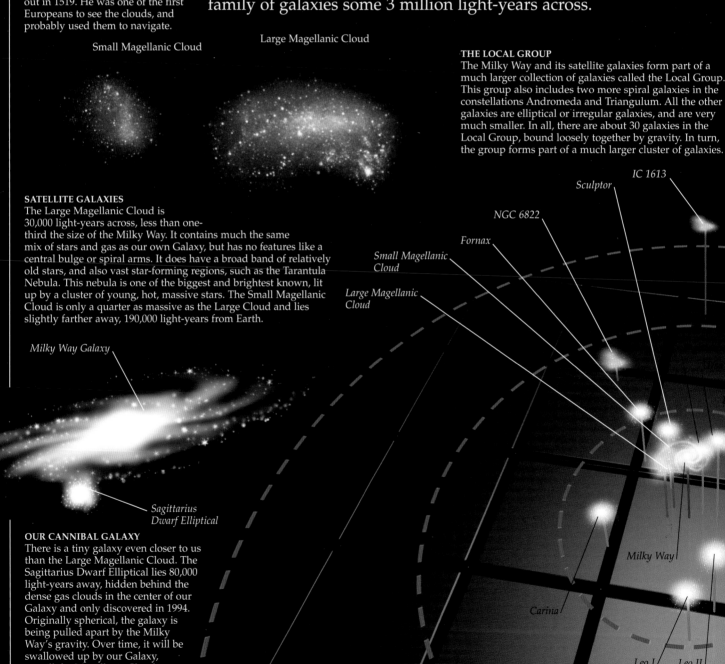

Milky Way Galaxy

Sagittarius Dwarf Elliptical

IC 1613

Sculptor

NGC 6822

Fornax

Small Magellanic Cloud

Large Magellanic Cloud

Milky Way

Carina

Leo I

Leo II

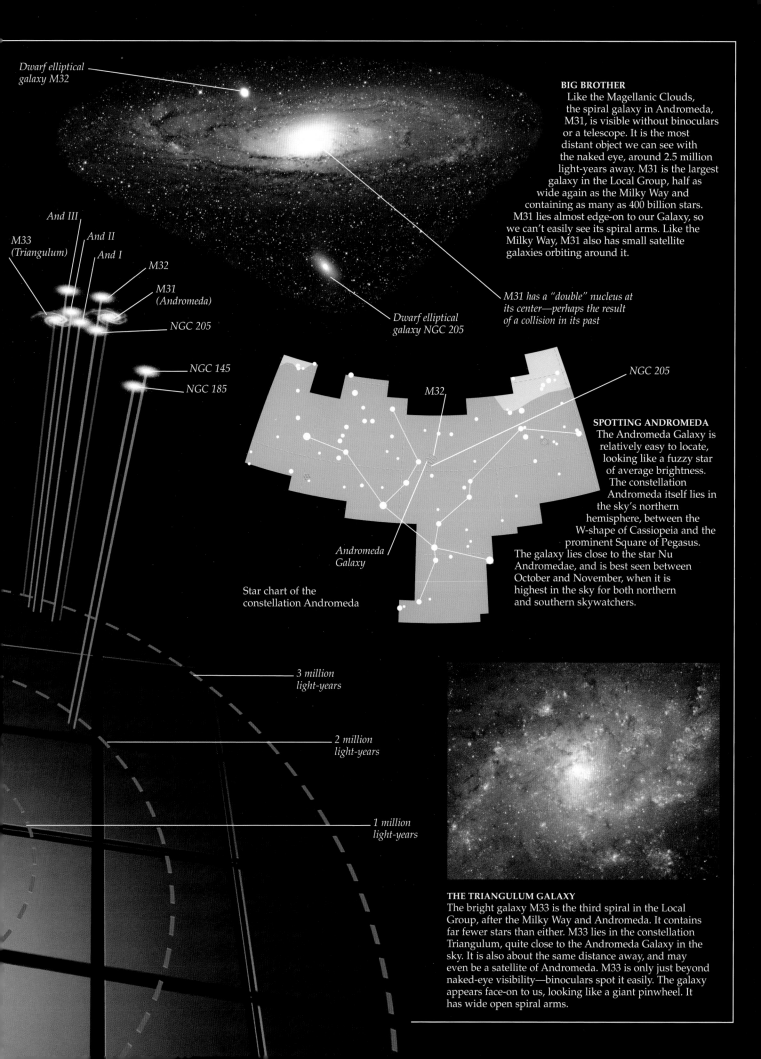

Dwarf elliptical
galaxy M32

BIG BROTHER
Like the Magellanic Clouds,
the spiral galaxy in Andromeda,
M31, is visible without binoculars
or a telescope. It is the most
distant object we can see with
the naked eye, around 2.5 million
light-years away. M31 is the largest
galaxy in the Local Group, half as
wide again as the Milky Way and
containing as many as 400 billion stars.
M31 lies almost edge-on to our Galaxy, so
we can't easily see its spiral arms. Like the
Milky Way, M31 also has small satellite
galaxies orbiting around it.

And III
And II
M33
(Triangulum)
And I
M32
M31
(Andromeda)
NGC 205

NGC 145
NGC 185

*M31 has a "double" nucleus at
its center—perhaps the result
of a collision in its past*

Dwarf elliptical
galaxy NGC 205

M32

NGC 205

SPOTTING ANDROMEDA
The Andromeda Galaxy is
relatively easy to locate,
looking like a fuzzy star
of average brightness.
The constellation
Andromeda itself lies in
the sky's northern
hemisphere, between the
W-shape of Cassiopeia and the
prominent Square of Pegasus.
The galaxy lies close to the star Nu
Andromedae, and is best seen between
October and November, when it is
highest in the sky for both northern
and southern skywatchers.

Andromeda
Galaxy

Star chart of the
constellation Andromeda

3 million
light-years

2 million
light-years

1 million
light-years

THE TRIANGULUM GALAXY
The bright galaxy M33 is the third spiral in the Local
Group, after the Milky Way and Andromeda. It contains
far fewer stars than either. M33 lies in the constellation
Triangulum, quite close to the Andromeda Galaxy in the
sky. It is also about the same distance away, and may
even be a satellite of Andromeda. M33 is only just beyond
naked-eye visibility—binoculars spot it easily. The galaxy
appears face-on to us, looking like a giant pinwheel. It
has wide open spiral arms.

Galaxies galore

THE MILKY WAY AND THE OTHER GALAXIES that make up the Local Group occupy only a tiny region of space, a few million light-years across. Scattered throughout the rest of space, across tens of billions of light-years, are tens of billions of other galaxies. Many are spiral in shape, like the Milky Way and the Andromeda Galaxy. Many are oval, or elliptical, and others have no regular shape at all. Some galaxies are dwarfs, with perhaps less than a million stars, but others are giants with hundreds of billions. Occasionally, galaxies create spectacular celestial fireworks as they crash into one another. Astronomers don't know exactly when galaxies started to form, but it was probably less than 2 billion years after the Universe itself was born.

COLLIDING GALAXIES
Relatively speaking, there is not a great deal of space between the galaxies—and, from time to time, they crash into one another. Usually, it is not the individual stars that collide but the vast gas clouds inside the galaxies. The crashing together of the clouds triggers off bouts of furious star formation, known as starbursts.

Stars are thrown out of both galaxies during collision

Elliptical galaxies classified E0–E9 in order of increasing ellipticity

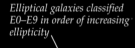

Spiral galaxy NGC 2207

Elliptical galaxies (E)

Spiral galaxies (S)

Barred spiral galaxies (SB)

Spirals and barred spirals classified Sa–Sc and SBa–SBc, depending on the structure of their arms

Colliding galaxies
NGC 2207 and IC 2163

HUBBLE'S TUNING FORK
Galaxy pioneer Edwin Hubble devised the method astronomers use to classify galaxies. He divided up regular galaxies into ellipticals (E), spirals (S), and barred spirals (SB), according to their shape, in his so-called tuning-fork diagram.

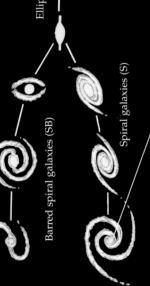

Starburst region—a vast stellar nursery

IRREGULAR GALAXIES
Galaxies with no particular shape are classed as irregulars. They are rich in gas and dust, with many young stars and plenty of star-forming regions. The Magellanic Clouds are irregulars, as is M82 in Ursa Major (left). M82 is crossed by prominent dark dust lanes and is undergoing a massive burst of star formation.

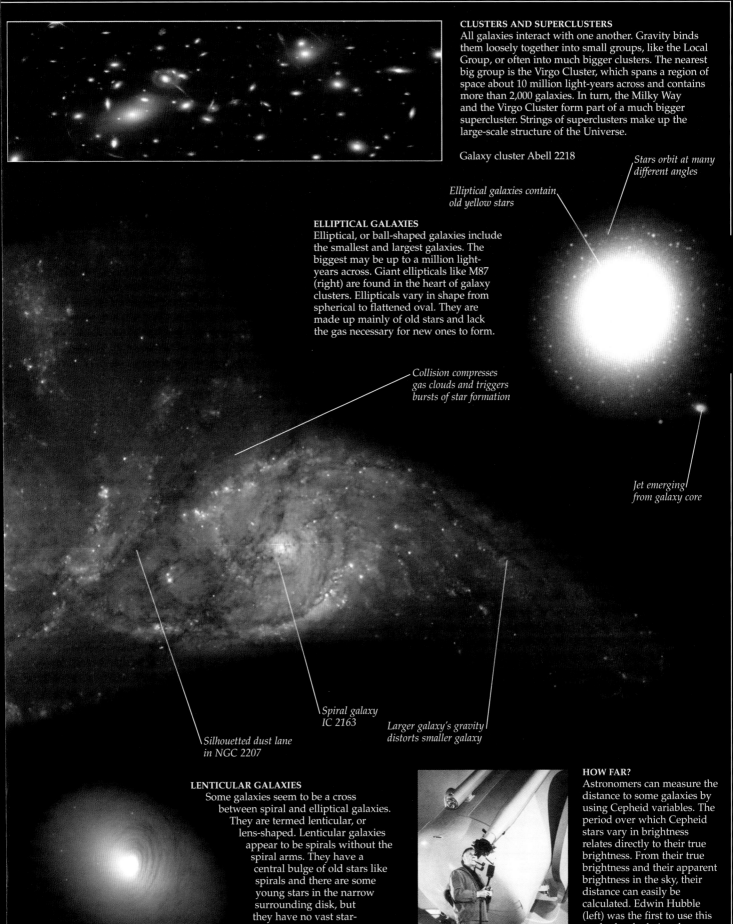

CLUSTERS AND SUPERCLUSTERS
All galaxies interact with one another. Gravity binds them loosely together into small groups, like the Local Group, or often into much bigger clusters. The nearest big group is the Virgo Cluster, which spans a region of space about 10 million light-years across and contains more than 2,000 galaxies. In turn, the Milky Way and the Virgo Cluster form part of a much bigger supercluster. Strings of superclusters make up the large-scale structure of the Universe.

Galaxy cluster Abell 2218

Stars orbit at many different angles

Elliptical galaxies contain old yellow stars

ELLIPTICAL GALAXIES
Elliptical, or ball-shaped galaxies include the smallest and largest galaxies. The biggest may be up to a million light-years across. Giant ellipticals like M87 (right) are found in the heart of galaxy clusters. Ellipticals vary in shape from spherical to flattened oval. They are made up mainly of old stars and lack the gas necessary for new ones to form.

Collision compresses gas clouds and triggers bursts of star formation

Jet emerging from galaxy core

Silhouetted dust lane in NGC 2207

Spiral galaxy IC 2163

Larger galaxy's gravity distorts smaller galaxy

LENTICULAR GALAXIES
Some galaxies seem to be a cross between spiral and elliptical galaxies. They are termed lenticular, or lens-shaped. Lenticular galaxies appear to be spirals without the spiral arms. They have a central bulge of old stars like spirals and there are some young stars in the narrow surrounding disk, but they have no vast star-forming regions.

Lenticular galaxy NGC 2787

HOW FAR?
Astronomers can measure the distance to some galaxies by using Cepheid variables. The period over which Cepheid stars vary in brightness relates directly to their true brightness. From their true brightness and their apparent brightness in the sky, their distance can easily be calculated. Edwin Hubble (left) was the first to use this method, calculating the distance to the Andromeda Galaxy in 1923.

Quasars and other active galaxies

MOST GALAXIES GIVE OUT THE ENERGY of hundreds of billions of stars shining together, but some give out much more. We call these active galaxies, and they include radio galaxies, quasars, blazars, and Seyfert galaxies. Quasars are perhaps the most intriguing of active galaxies. Their name is short for "quasi-stellar radio source," because they look like faint stars and give off radio waves. But quasars have enormous red shifts, and so must lie billions of light-years away, far beyond the stars. Powerful telescopes reveal that they are in fact galaxies with very bright centers. To be visible at such distances, quasars must be hundreds of times brighter than normal galaxies, but rapid changes in their brightness mean that most of their light must be generated in a region little larger than our Solar System. Today, astronomers think that quasars and other active galaxies get their energy from massive black holes at their centers.

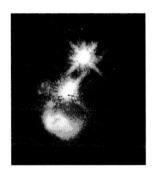

LOOKING AT QUASARS
A former assistant to Edwin Hubble, US astronomer Allan Sandage (born 1926) helped discover quasars. In 1960, he linked radio source 3C48 with a faint starlike object but could not explain its spectrum. It was three years before 3C48 was identified as a quasar with a large red shift.

RADIO GALAXIES
NGC 5128 in the constellation Centaurus is an elliptical galaxy cut in two by a dark band of obscuring dust. It houses a powerful radio source called Centaurus A, and is the nearest active galaxy to us, just 15 million light-years away. This picture combines optical, X-ray (blue) and radio (red and green) views of the central region. A halo of X-ray-emitting gas surrounds the galaxy and a jet shoots out from its center, billowing out into huge radio-emitting lobes.

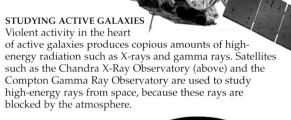

Camera

Polished metal mirror assembly used to reflect and focus X-rays

Solar panels

STUDYING ACTIVE GALAXIES
Violent activity in the heart of active galaxies produces copious amounts of high-energy radiation such as X-rays and gamma rays. Satellites such as the Chandra X-Ray Observatory (above) and the Compton Gamma Ray Observatory are used to study high-energy rays from space, because these rays are blocked by the atmosphere.

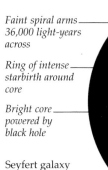

DISTANT QUASARS
The Hubble Space Telescope has spotted this quasar in the constellation Sculptor, emitting radiation as visible light. The quasar's powerful energy emission is fueled by a collision between two galaxies—the remains of one spiral ring lie just below the quasar itself. The quasar lies 3 billion light-years away—a much closer star shines just above it.

Faint spiral arms 36,000 light-years across

Ring of intense starbirth around core

Bright core powered by black hole

Seyfert galaxy NGC 7742

SEYFERT GALAXIES
Some spiral galaxies have particularly bright centers and are classed as Seyfert galaxies after US astronomer Carl Seyfert, who first noticed them in 1943. They are now thought to be closer and less powerful versions of quasars. About one in 10 large spiral galaxies appear to be Seyferts, and our own Milky Way may become one in time.

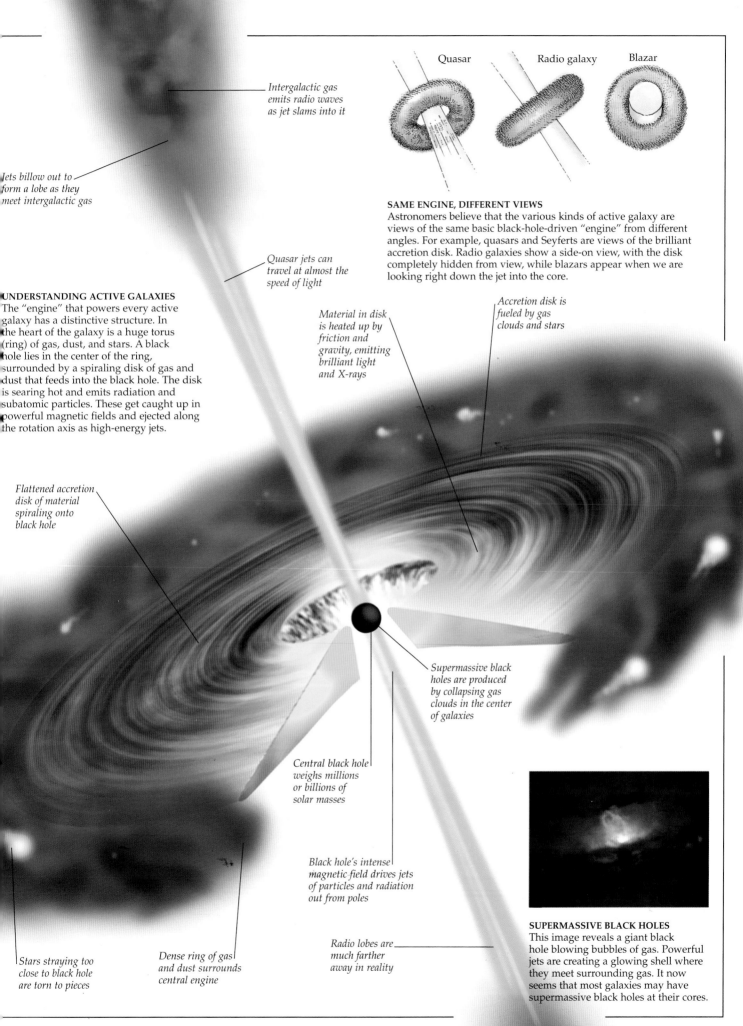

Intergalactic gas emits radio waves as jet slams into it

Jets billow out to form a lobe as they meet intergalactic gas

Quasar Radio galaxy Blazar

SAME ENGINE, DIFFERENT VIEWS
Astronomers believe that the various kinds of active galaxy are views of the same basic black-hole-driven "engine" from different angles. For example, quasars and Seyferts are views of the brilliant accretion disk. Radio galaxies show a side-on view, with the disk completely hidden from view, while blazars appear when we are looking right down the jet into the core.

Quasar jets can travel at almost the speed of light

UNDERSTANDING ACTIVE GALAXIES
The "engine" that powers every active galaxy has a distinctive structure. In the heart of the galaxy is a huge torus (ring) of gas, dust, and stars. A black hole lies in the center of the ring, surrounded by a spiraling disk of gas and dust that feeds into the black hole. The disk is searing hot and emits radiation and subatomic particles. These get caught up in powerful magnetic fields and ejected along the rotation axis as high-energy jets.

Material in disk is heated up by friction and gravity, emitting brilliant light and X-rays

Accretion disk is fueled by gas clouds and stars

Flattened accretion disk of material spiraling onto black hole

Supermassive black holes are produced by collapsing gas clouds in the center of galaxies

Central black hole weighs millions or billions of solar masses

Black hole's intense magnetic-field drives jets of particles and radiation out from poles

Stars straying too close to black hole are torn to pieces

Dense ring of gas and dust surrounds central engine

Radio lobes are much farther away in reality

SUPERMASSIVE BLACK HOLES
This image reveals a giant black hole blowing bubbles of gas. Powerful jets are creating a glowing shell where they meet surrounding gas. It now seems that most galaxies may have supermassive black holes at their cores.

A Universe of life

Our planet teems with life in extraordinary variety, but we know of no other place in the Solar System or even in the Universe where life exists. Surely there must be other life "out there." There are billions of stars like the Sun in our Galaxy alone, and some of them must have planets capable of supporting life. And on some of these worlds, intelligent life should arise, capable of communicating across space. Since the 1960s, various projects have been set up to conduct the search for extraterrestrial intelligence (SETI) using radio telescopes. It seems likely that aliens would use radio waves of some sort to communicate, just as we do.

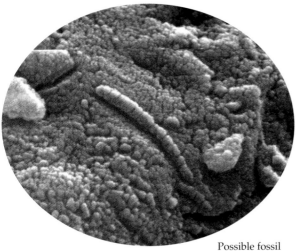

Crab on a black smoker

EXTREMES OF LIFE
Scientists used to think that life could only arise in mild conditions like those on Earth's surface, but recent discoveries of creatures in extreme environments have changed their minds. Animals even thrive on the deep-sea floor around black smokers—volcanic vents spewing out sulfur-laden water at 660°F (350°C).

Possible fossil bacteria in Martian meteorite

LIFE IN THE SOLAR SYSTEM?
Mars has long been considered as a place where life of some sort might exist, either now or in the past. The planet is inhospitable to life now, but it probably had a more suitable climate long ago. If life gained a foothold at that time, it could have left fossils in the Martian soil. In 1996, NASA scientists thought they had found traces of ancient life in a meteorite that came from Mars, but others were skeptical.

HARBINGERS OF LIFE
Many carbon-based, organic molecules have been found in the gas clouds that exist between the stars. There are even simple amino acids, which are essential building blocks for life. This suggests that life might be common in the Universe. It could be spread through solar systems by the most primitive of celestial bodies—the comets.

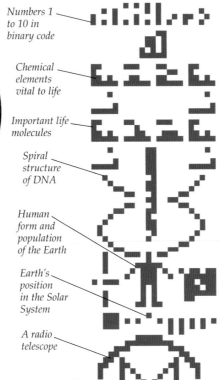

Numbers 1 to 10 in binary code

Chemical elements vital to life

Important life molecules

Spiral structure of DNA

Human form and population of the Earth

Earth's position in the Solar System

A radio telescope

TALKING TO ALIENS
The only message mankind has so far deliberately sent to aliens was transmitted in digital form as a set of 1,679 on–off pulses. This number is the result of multiplying two prime numbers, 23 and 73, and the message becomes clear when laid out in 73 rows of 23 columns. With black squares for 1s and white squares for 0s, a pattern or pictogram is produced and forms a message.

ARECIBO CALLING
The message (left) was transmitted from the huge Arecibo radio telescope in 1974. It was beamed at a globular cluster of 300,000 stars, increasing the possibility of reaching intelligent life. But the signal won't reach its target for another 25,000 years.

INTERSTELLAR MESSAGES
The *Pioneer 10* and *11* and *Voyager 1* and 2 space probes are now winging their way out of the Solar System carrying messages for aliens. The *Pioneers* carry pictorial plaques; the *Voyagers* have gold phonograph disks on which typical sights and sounds of Earth are recorded.

THE CHANCES OF LIFE

US radio astronomer Frank Drake (born 1930) pioneered the use of radio telescopes to listen for signals from aliens. He also devised an equation (left) that estimates how many advanced civilizations within our Galaxy should be able and willing to communicate with us. Unfortunately, we still don't know enough about our Universe to use the Drake Equation properly.

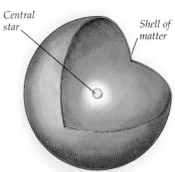

Central star

Shell of matter

SIGNS OF INTELLIGENCE

US physicist Freeman Dyson has suggested that an advanced civilization would remodel its corner of the Universe, perhaps building a huge sphere around its star to trap energy. We could detect civilizations by looking for distinctive emissions from these "Dyson spheres."

WHAT MIGHT THEY BE LIKE?

It is almost impossible to guess what alien life would be like, but biologists can make educated guesses based on the principle of evolution. Simply put, this means that any creature must be well-suited to its environment in order to survive and pass on its characteristics to another generation. Using this principle, we can imagine viable aliens like this low-browsing herbivore from Epsilon Reticuli b.

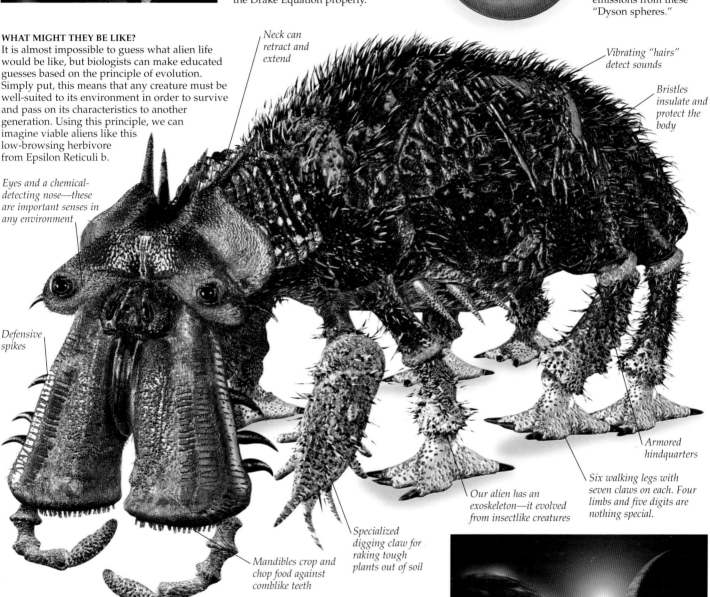

Neck can retract and extend

Vibrating "hairs" detect sounds

Bristles insulate and protect the body

Eyes and a chemical-detecting nose—these are important senses in any environment

Defensive spikes

Armored hindquarters

Six walking legs with seven claws on each. Four limbs and five digits are nothing special.

Our alien has an exoskeleton—it evolved from insectlike creatures

Specialized digging claw for raking tough plants out of soil

Mandibles crop and chop food against comblike teeth

CULTURE SHOCK

Some people believe that aliens are already visiting Earth and making contact with humans, but most think we have yet to make our first contact with alien intelligence. If and when that happens, the impact on humankind will be enormous. The clash in physical form and culture would be infinitely more shocking than when Columbus first met Native Americans in 1472 (left), and could be as damaging for our species as it was for the Native Americans.

EPSILON RETICULI

The hypothetical alien above comes from a moon of the giant planet Epsilon Reticuli b, about 60 light-years from Earth. The planet, discovered in 2000, orbits its star just 20 percent farther out than Earth orbits the Sun. The star Epsilon Reticuli itself seems to be a Sunlike star just starting to evolve into its red giant phase.

Index

Acknowledgements

Dorling Kindersley would like to thank:

Epsilon Reticuli b alien:
Darren Naish, Mark Longworth

Other commissioned illustrations:
Peter Bull

DK Pictures:
Jonathan Brooks, Sarah Mills

Picture credits:

The publisher would like to thank the following for their kind permission to reproduce their photographs:

a=above; b=below; c=centre; l=left; r=right; t=top;

Agence France Presse: 52bl; **AKG London:** 39tr, 45br; Cameraphoto 40tl; **Anglo-Australian Observatory:** David Malin 51tr; **The Art Archive:** Musée du Louvre Paris /

Dagli Orti (A) 27cr; **Bridgeman Art Library, London / New York:** Archives Charmet 47br; **British Museum:** 6bl; © **CERN Geneva:** 2tr, 10bl; **Corbis:** 62bc; Lucien Aigner 14tl; Yann Arthus-Bertrand 8cl; Bettmann 3tl, 7tr, 12bl, 18tl, 32cl, 59br; Dennis di Cicco 40-41c; Paul Hardy 14clb; Araldo de Luca 20tl; NASA 8clb, 39br; Michael Neveux 4cr, 6c; Robert Y. Ono 45bl; Enzo & Paolo Ragazzini 6bc; Roger Ressmeyer 4cl, 13tl, 17tr, 62cr; Paul A. Souders 29tr; Stapleton Collection 45cr; Brenda Tharp 53cla; Robert Yin 29br; **European Space Agency:** 11crb; ISO/ ISOCAM/ Alain Abergel 11br; NASA 40c; **Mary Evans Picture Library:** 8tl, 26bc, 27crb, 31br, 33br, 41cr, 56tl, 63bl; Alvin Correa 31br; **Galaxy Picture Library:** 25tl, 56cl, 57c, 57br, 59cra; **Getty Images:** Barros & Barros 12tl; **Sean Hunter:** 29cra; **Kobal Collection:** Universal 22c; **FLPA - Images of nature:** B Borrell 22cb, 22crb; **NASA:** 2b, 2cl, 3c, 3tr, 5tr, 9c, 9bl (x6), 11tl, 16br, 17br, 18cl, 18c, 19tr, 23tr, 23ca, 23cr, 23br, 26, 27tr, 27br, 27br, 27l, 29cr, 30br, 31cr, 31ac,

33tl, 33bl, 35cra, 35bl, 35bc, 35ac, 37cr, 38-39c, 50-51b, 55br; Craig Atteebery 35br; AURA/STScI 49tr; Boomerang Project 13c; Carnegie Mellon University 39cr; W.N. Colley and E. Turner (Princeton University), J.A. Tyson (Bell Labs, Lucent Technologies) 15cr; CXC / ASU/J 52c; ESA and The Hubble Heritage Team (STScI / AURA) 47bc; HST Comet Science Team 32bc; Institute of Space and Astronautical Sciences, Japan 21tr; JHUAPL 39tl, 39tc; JPL 8ca, 32c, 32bl, 33tc, 33cra, 33c, 33ac, 36clb, 36bc; JPL/University of Arizona 32-33; JSC 62cl; NOAO, ESA and The Hubble Heritage Team (STScI / AURA) 47tr; SOHO 20bl; Courtesy of SOHO / Extreme Ultraviolet Imaging Telescope (EIT) consortium 21bl; STScI 7bc, 9tr, 43tl, 48b, 49cr, 49br, 58-59c, 59tc, 59bl, 60cl, 60bl, 60br, 61br; STScI/ COBE/DIRBE Science Team 8bl; TRW 60cr; Dr. Hal Weaver and T. Ed Smith (STScI) 40bl; **Musee de la Poste, Paris, France:** 37c; **National Maritime Museum:** 4tr, 7cra, 43bc; **NOAA:** OAR / National Undersea Research Program (NURP) 62tcl; **NOAO / AURA / NSF:** N.A.Sharp 58; **Pikaia:** 2cra, 2crb, 4tl, 6-7, 9cl, 12bc, 14bl, 14-15, 15br, 24-25, 26tr, 27tc, 29cc, 30l, 31tr, 31cl, 36l, 37tc, 37bc, 37br, 44bl, 48tl,

49tl, 52cl, 53b, 56bl, 61c, 62bl, 62br; **Science Photo Library:** 10cl, 31bl, 31bl, 34br, 38bl; Michael Abbey 39bl; Estate of Francis Bello 60tl; Lawrence Berkeley Laboratory 15crb; Dr Eli Brinks 55tr; Chris Butler 18bl; Celestial Image Co 47c; Luke Dodd 46bl; Bernhard Edmaier 28cl; Dr Fred Espenak 6-7, 8-9, 26bl; Mark Garlick 19tl, 43tr; D.Golimowski, S.Durrance & M.Clampin 49cl; Hale Observatories 52tr; David A Hardy 12-13, 36c, 51br; Harvard College Observatory 19br, 43br; Claus Lunau/FOCI/Bonnier Publications 41bl; Maddox, Sutherland, Efstathiou & Loveday 9br; Allan Morton / Dennis Milon 54bl; MPIA-HD, Birkle, Slawik 7cr, 57tc; NASA 13tr, 28bl, 44bc; National Optical Astronomy Observatories 21cra; Novosti Press Agency 41br; Ludek Pesek 34cl; Detlev Van Ravenswaaj 38cl; Royal Observatory, Edinburgh / AAO 46-47; Rev. Ronald Royer 20-21t; John Sanford 16bl, 42crb; Robin Scagell 52br; Dan Schechter 14cl; Dr Seth Shostak 63tl; Joe Tucciarone 54-55c.

All other images © Dorling Kindersley.
For further information see:
www.dkimages.com